I0467862

Mandala
Creative Coloring

Copyright: Published in the United States Peter Raymond
Published April 2016
ISBN-13: 978-1530873128
ISBN-10: 1530873126

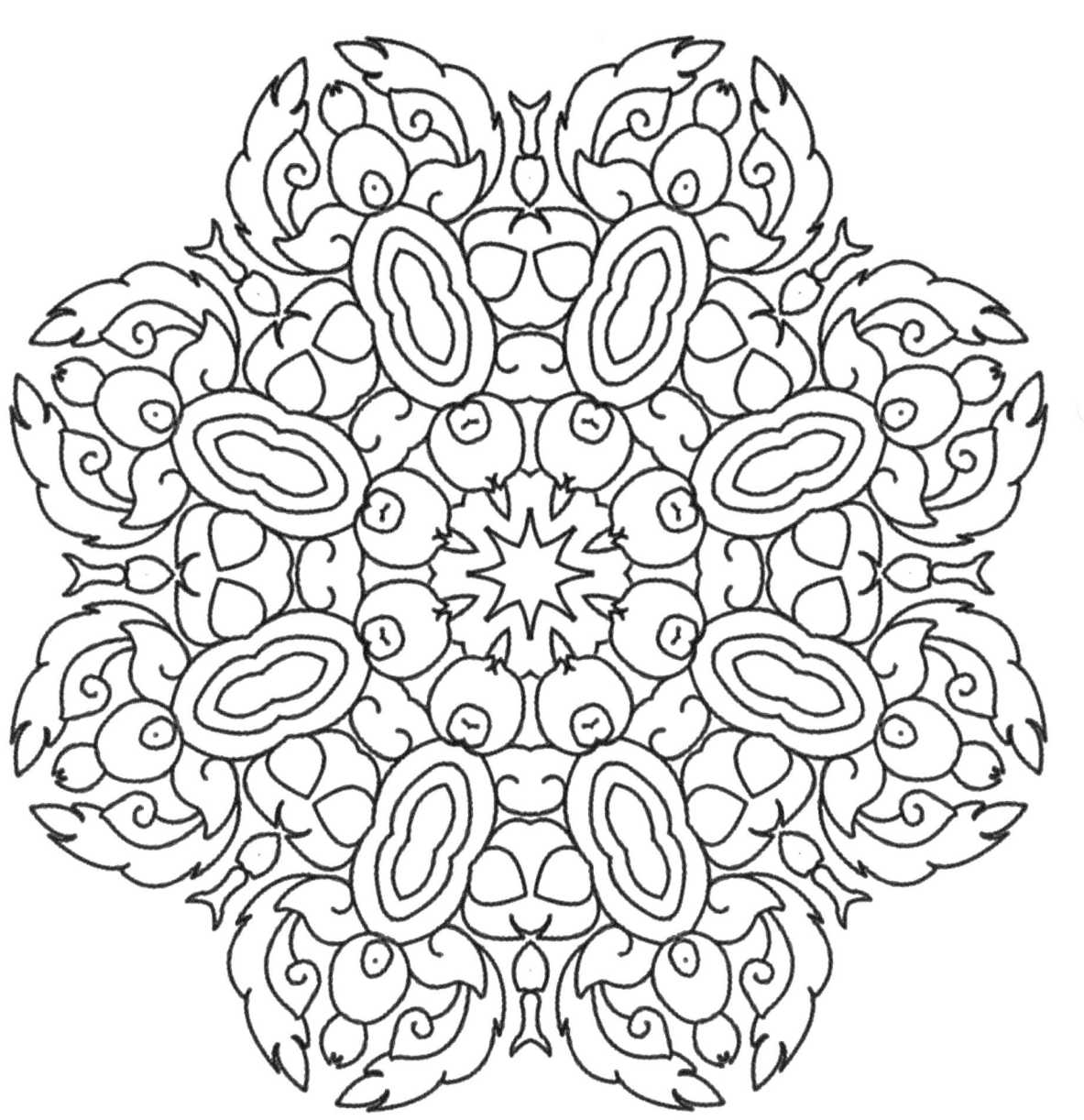

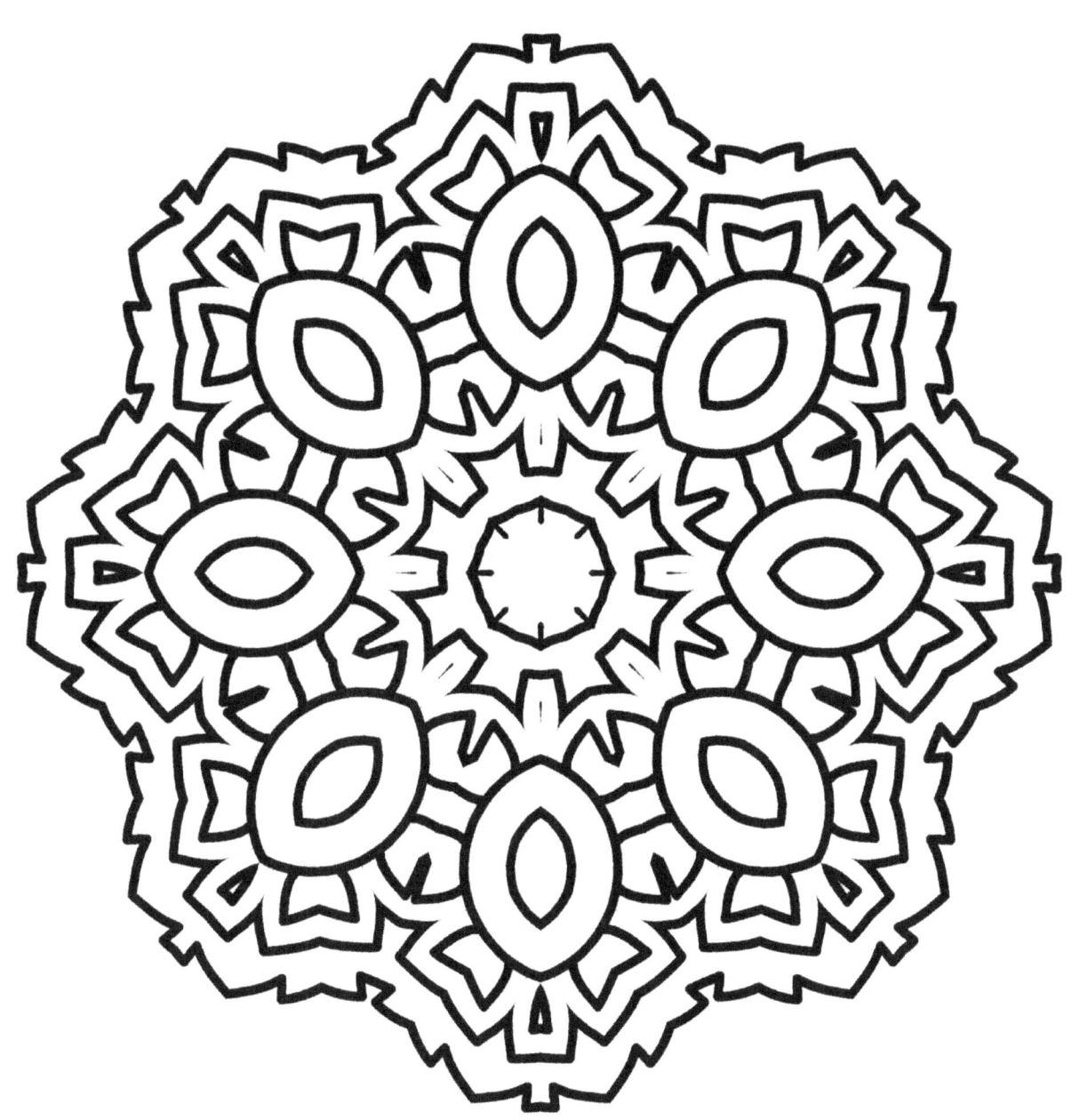

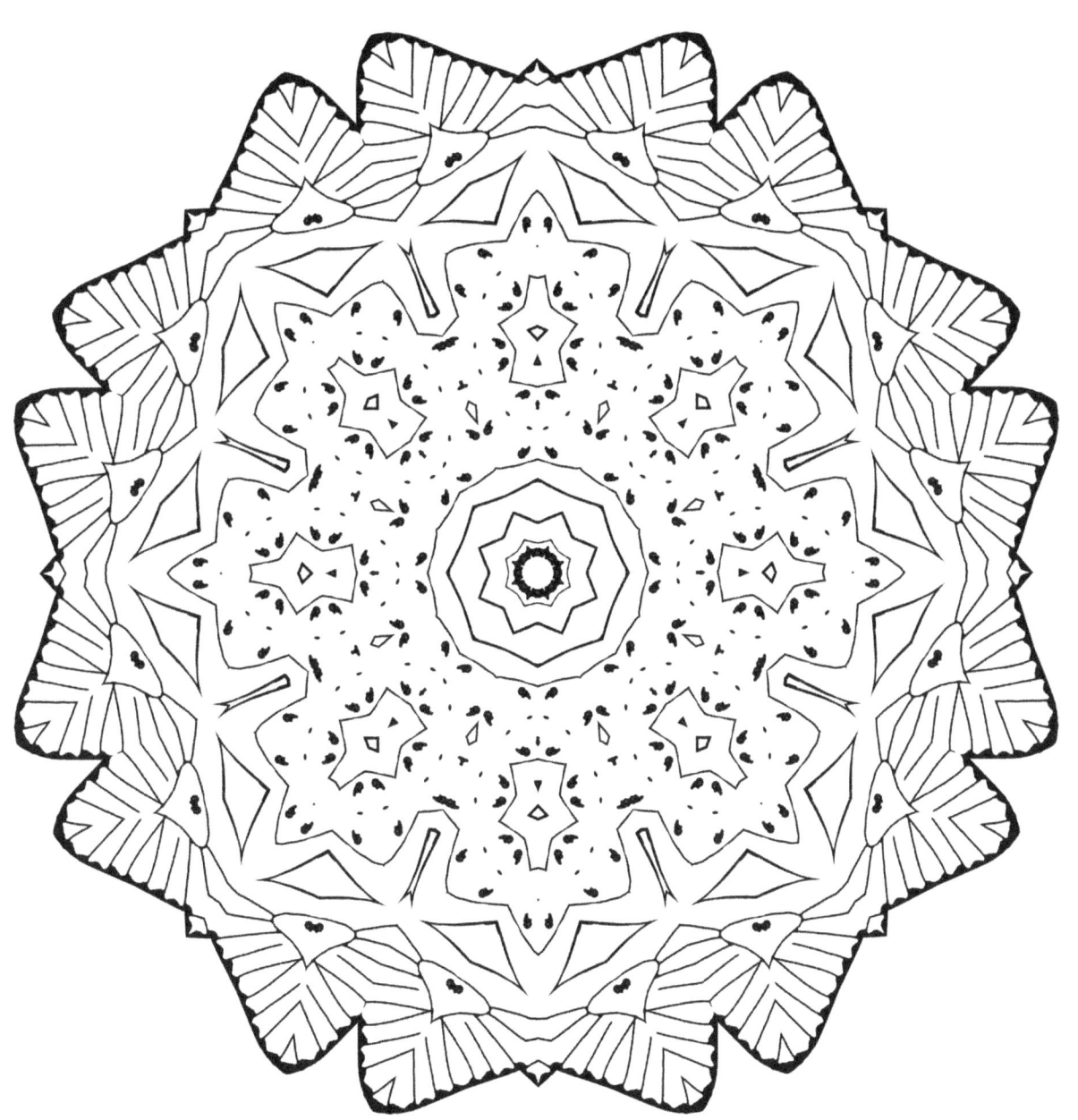

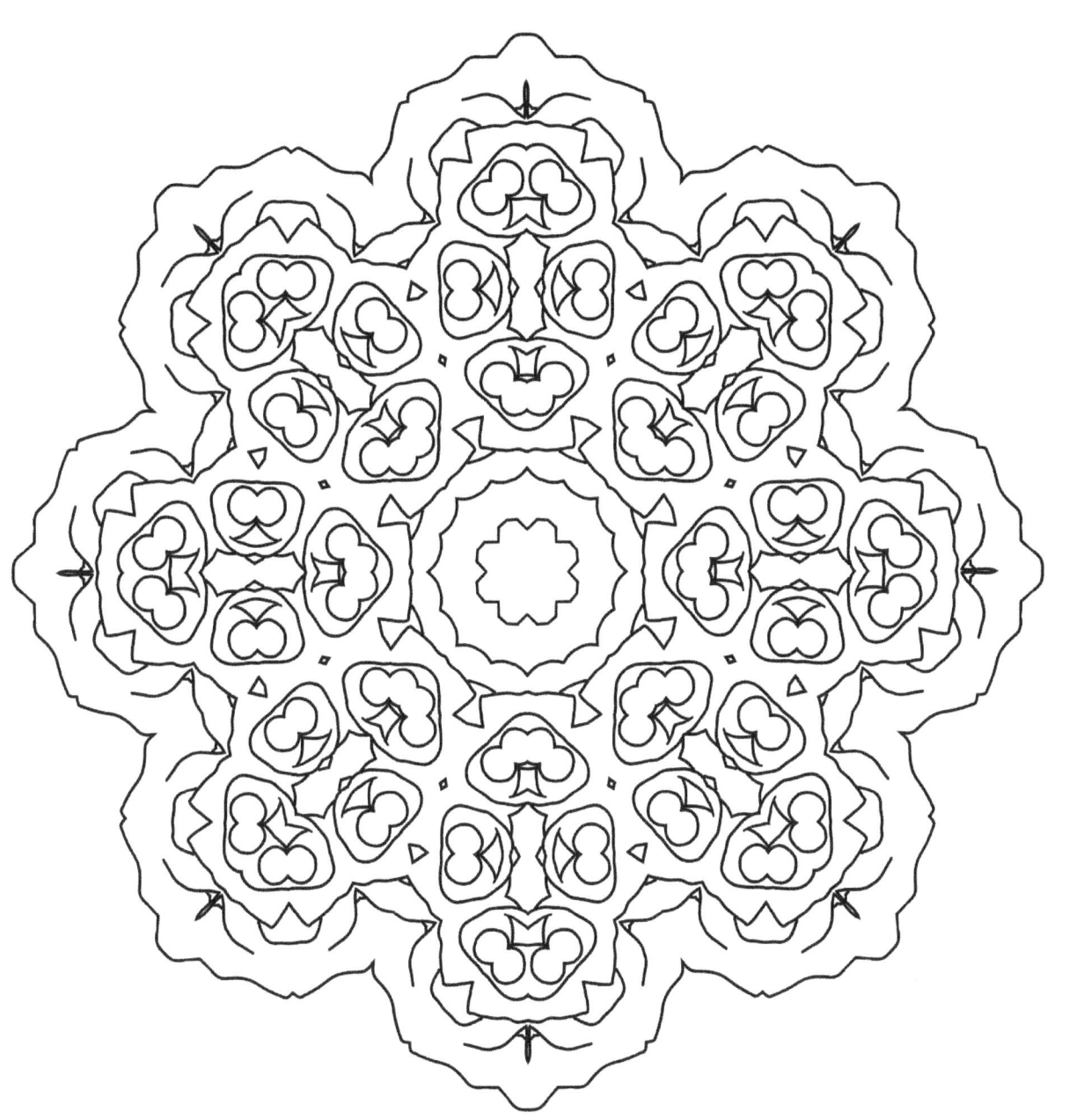

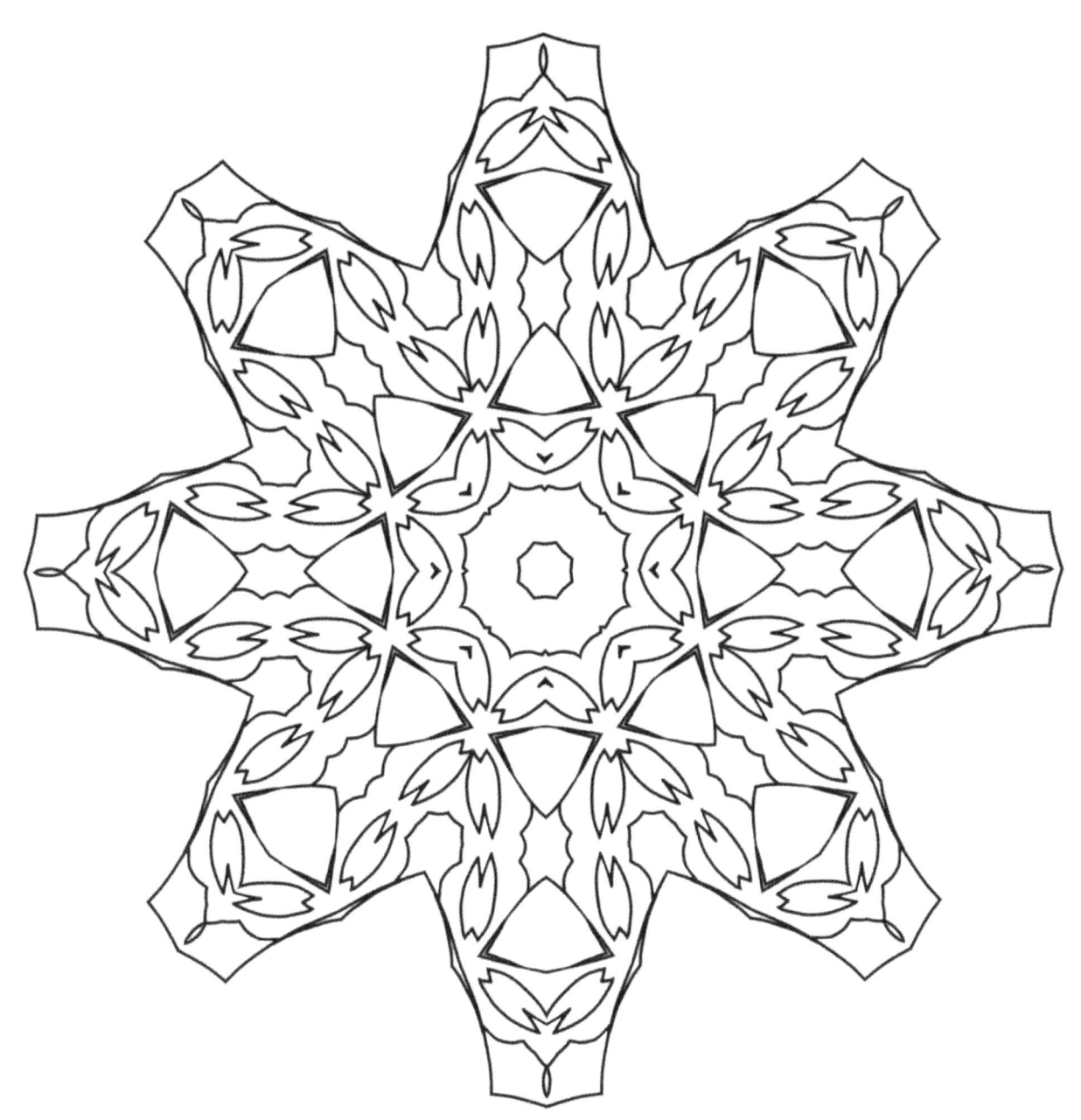

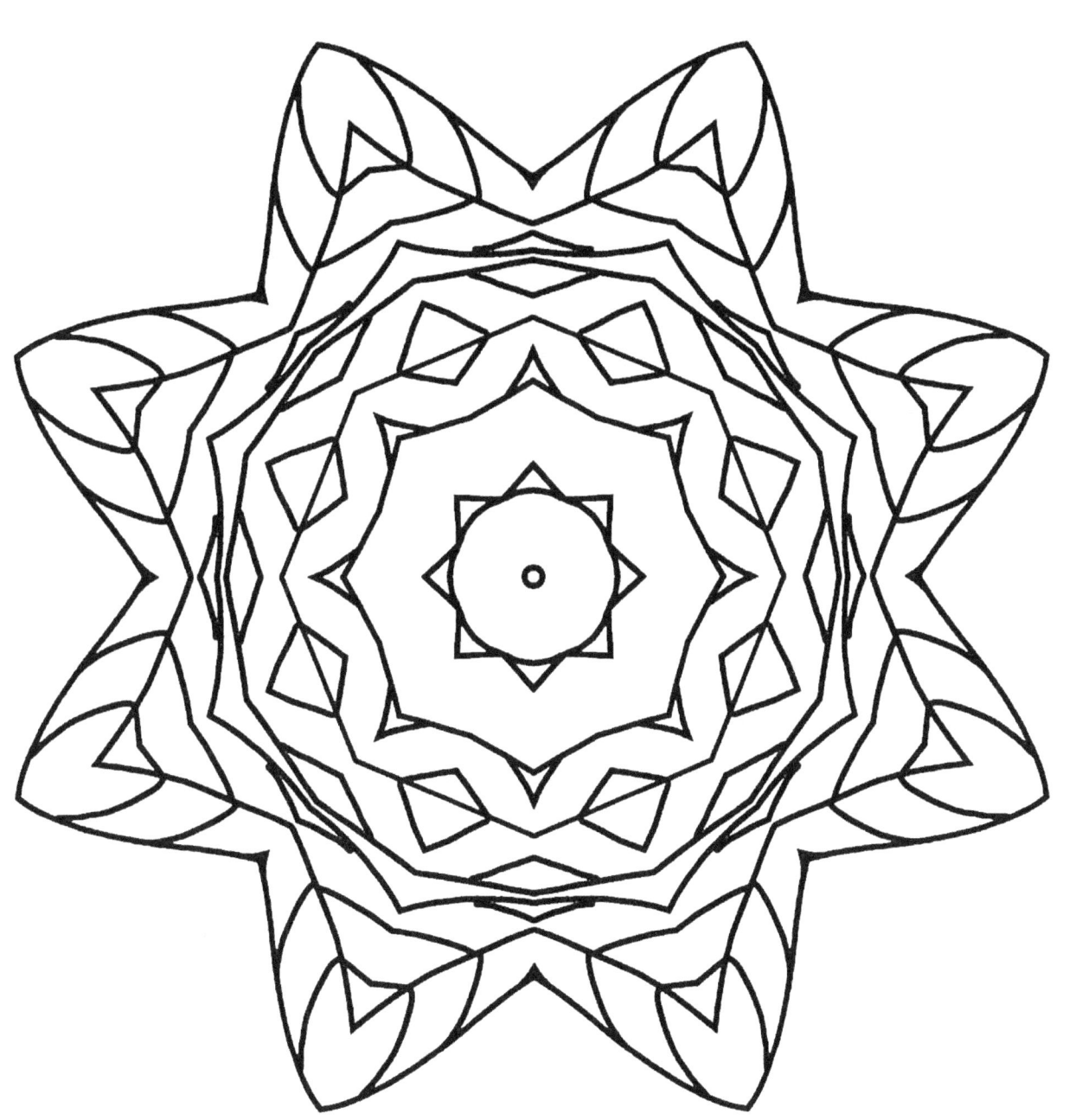

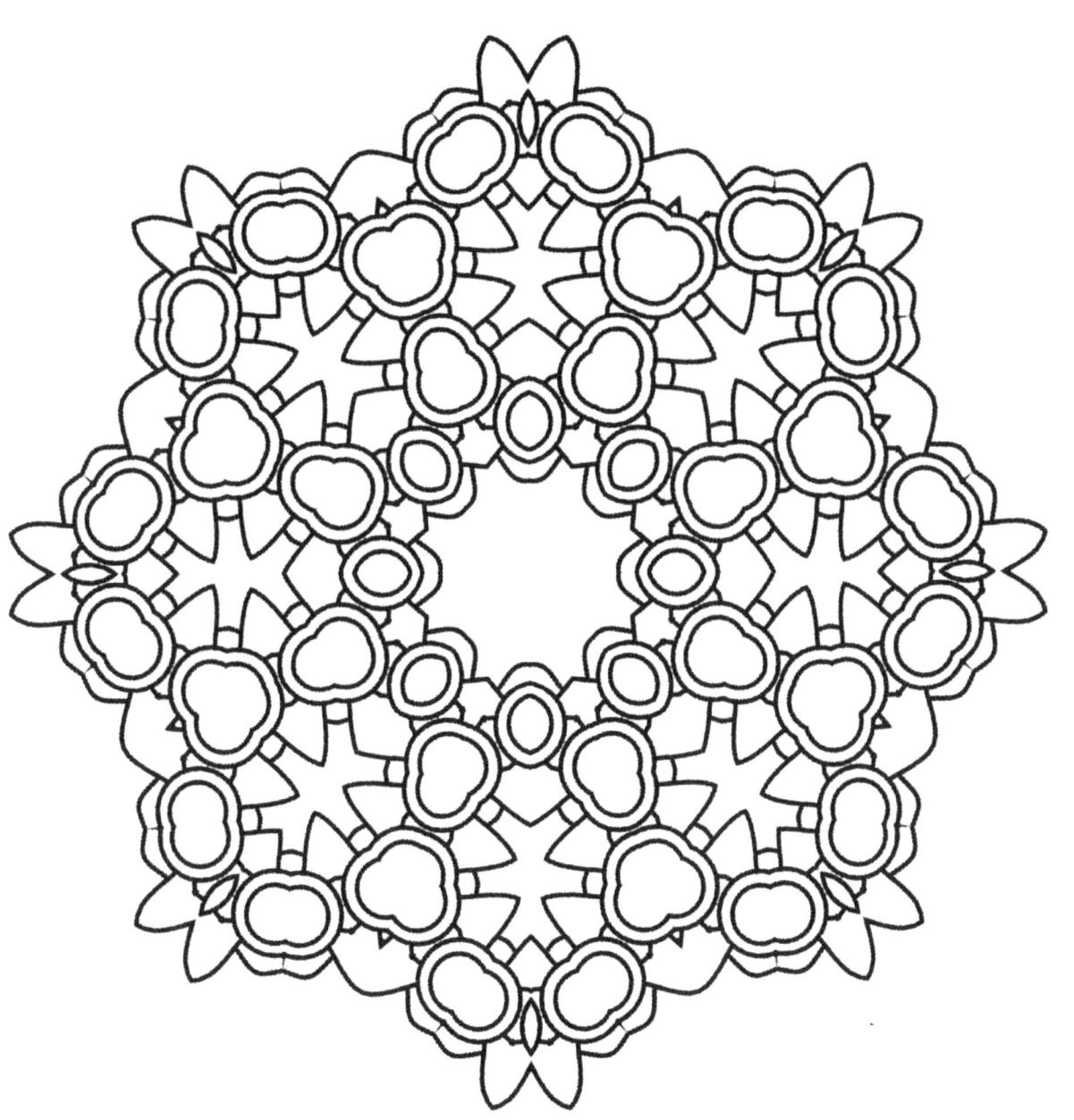

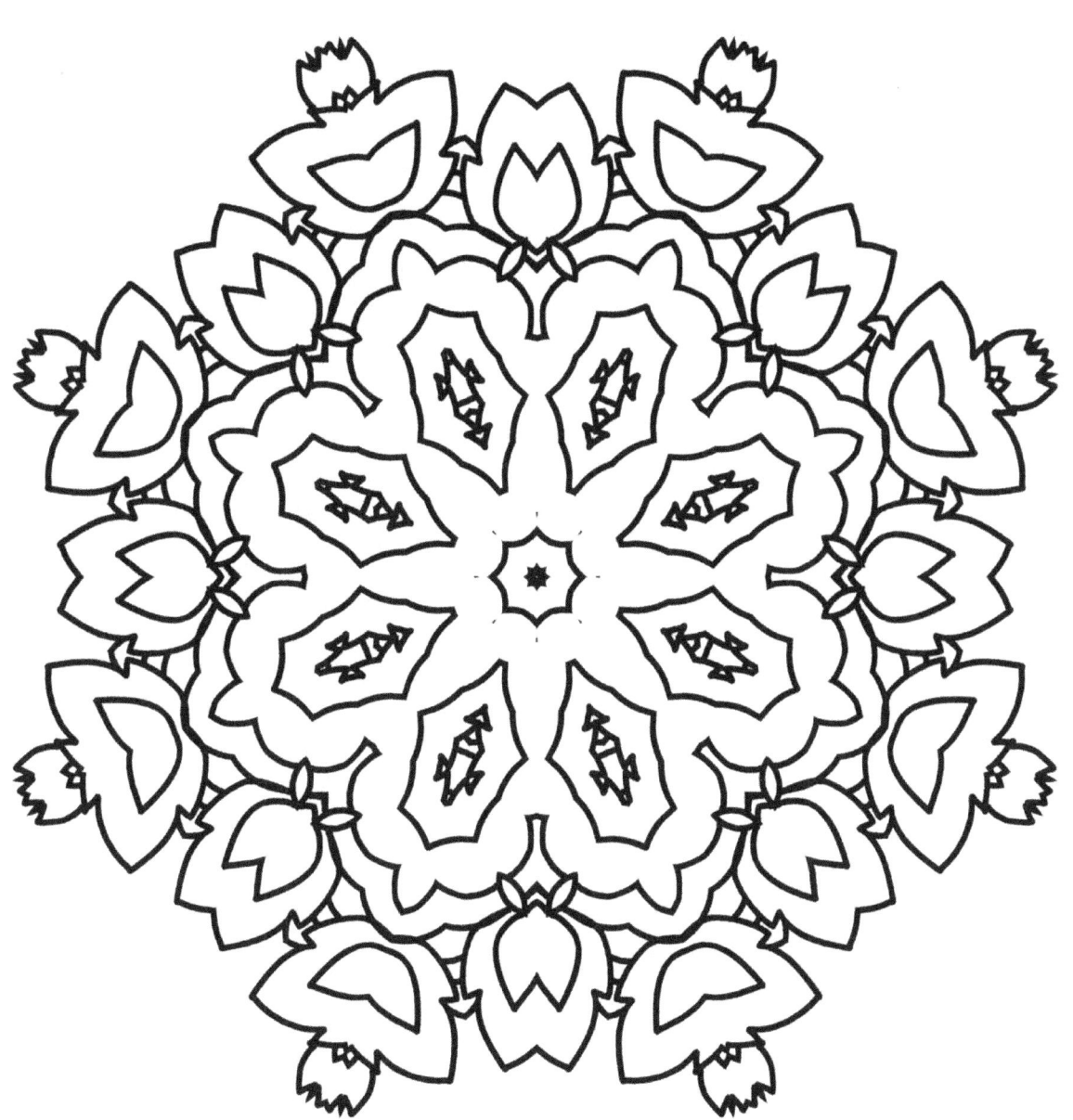

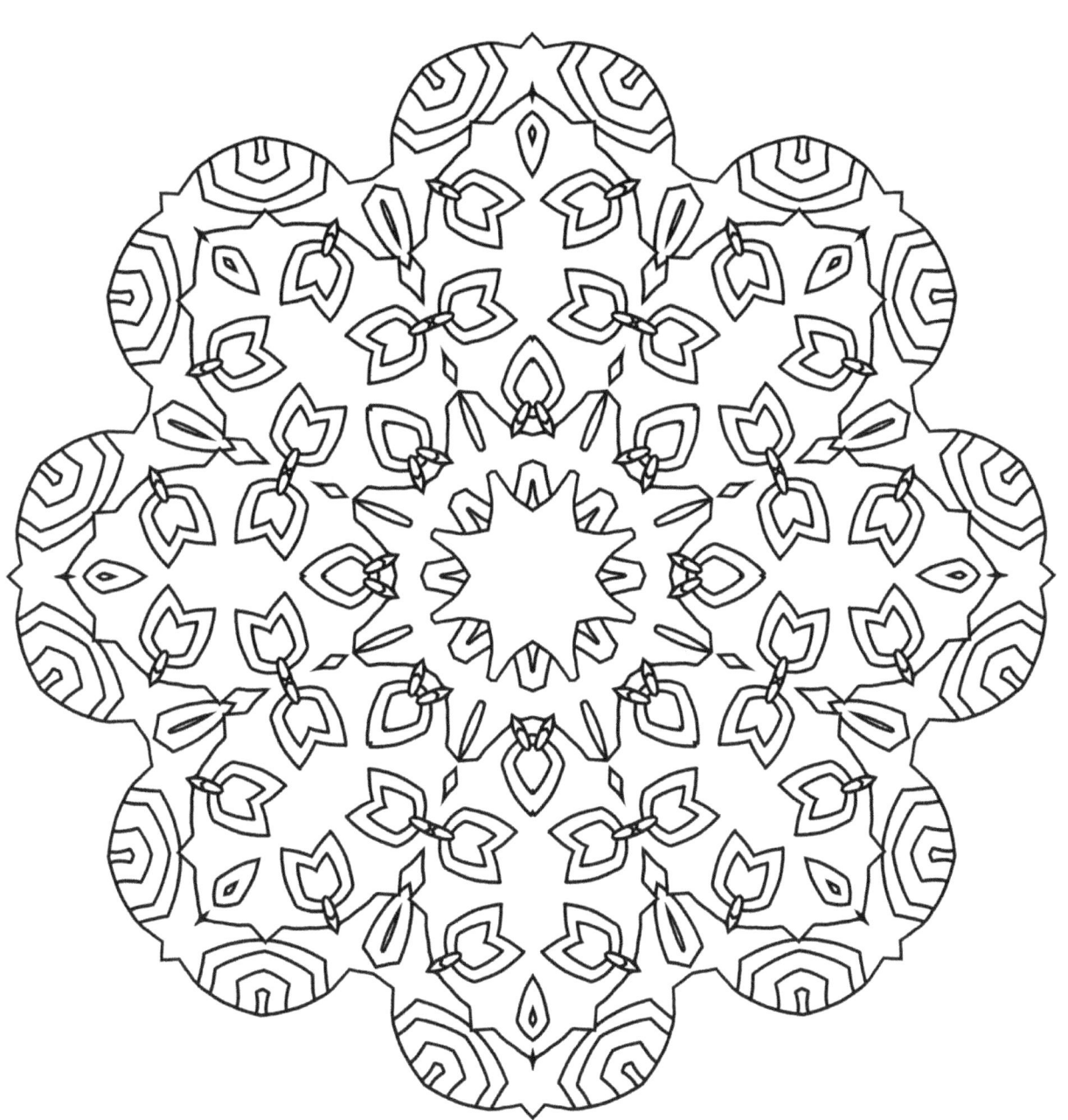

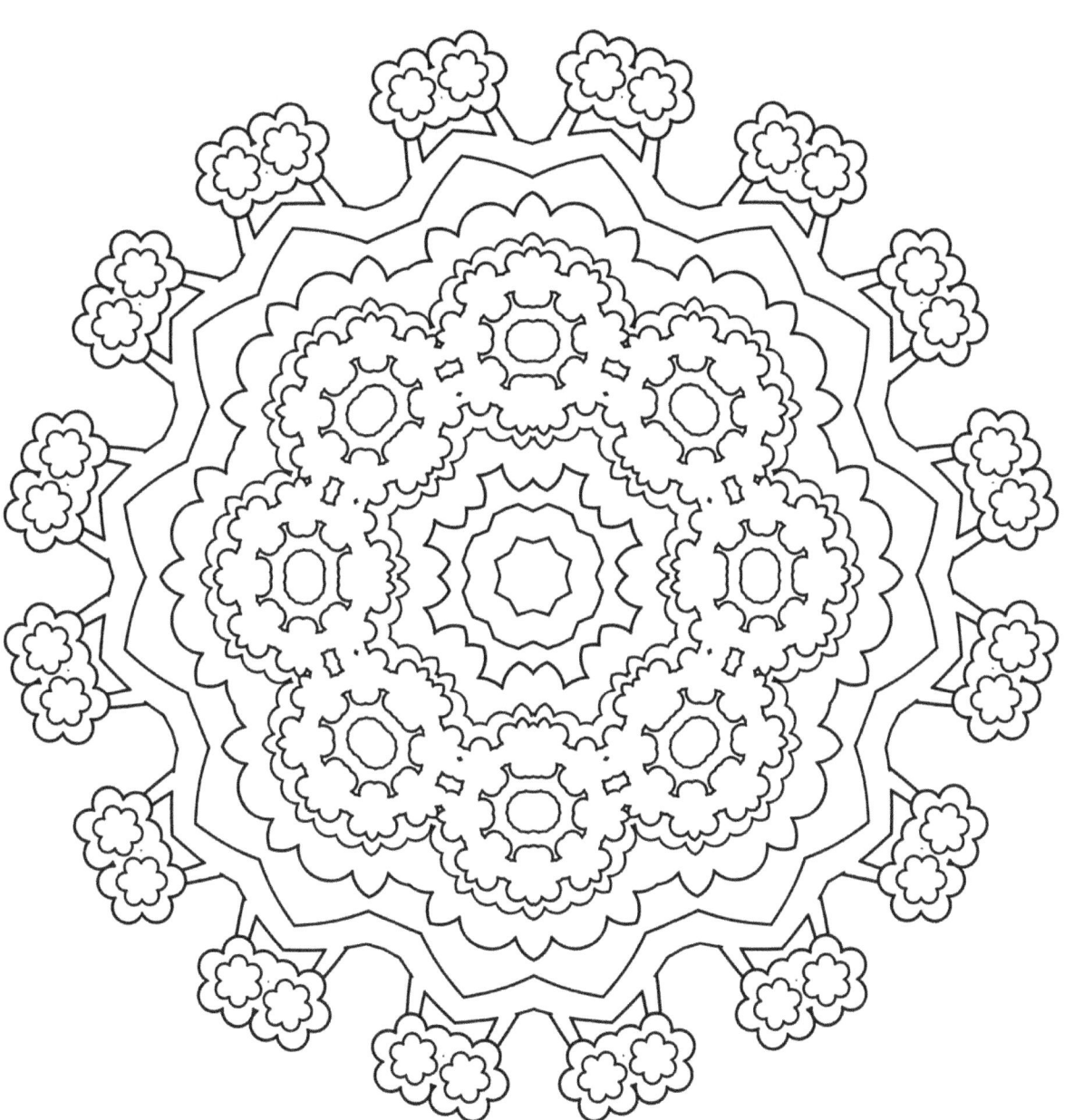

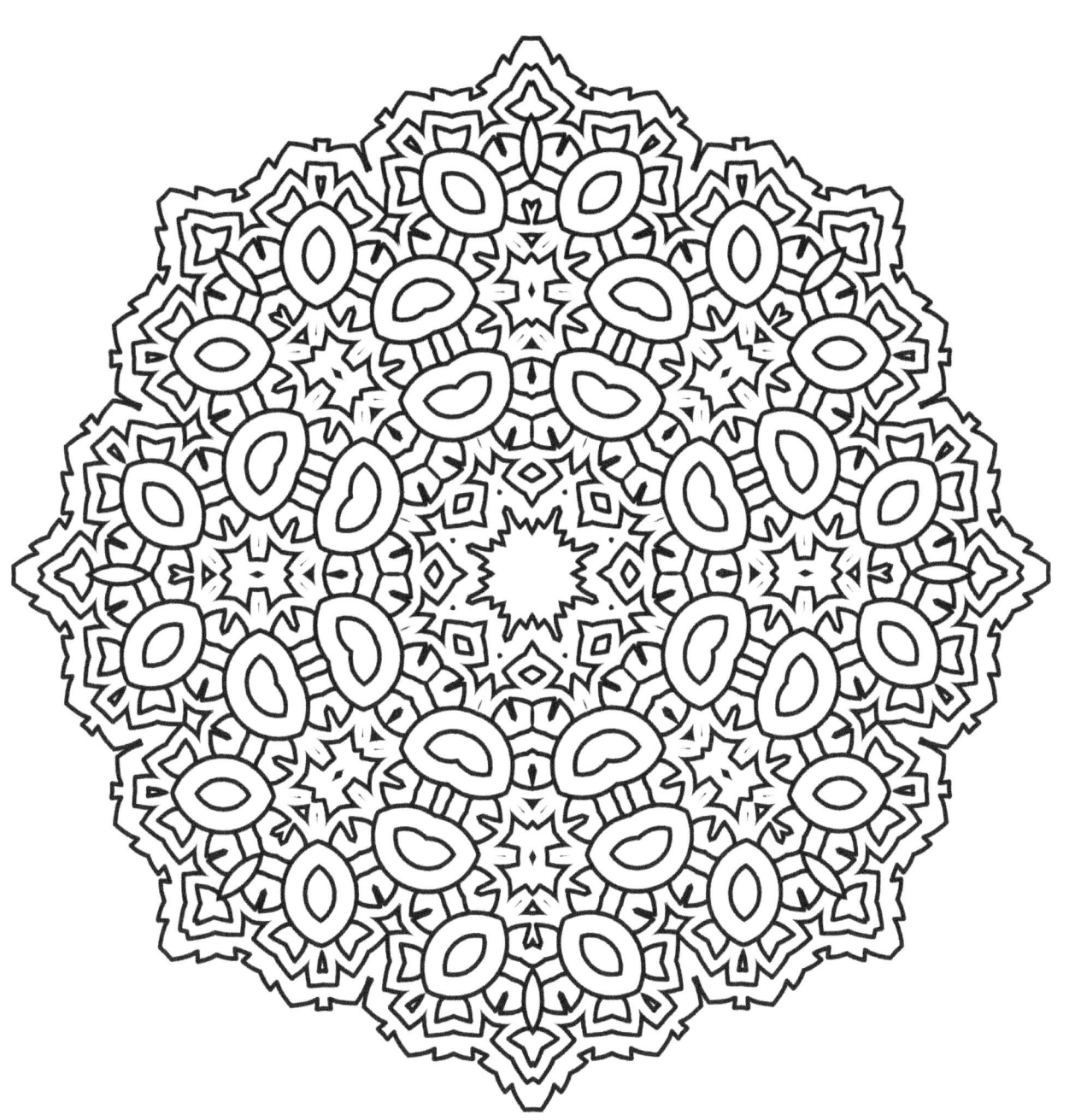

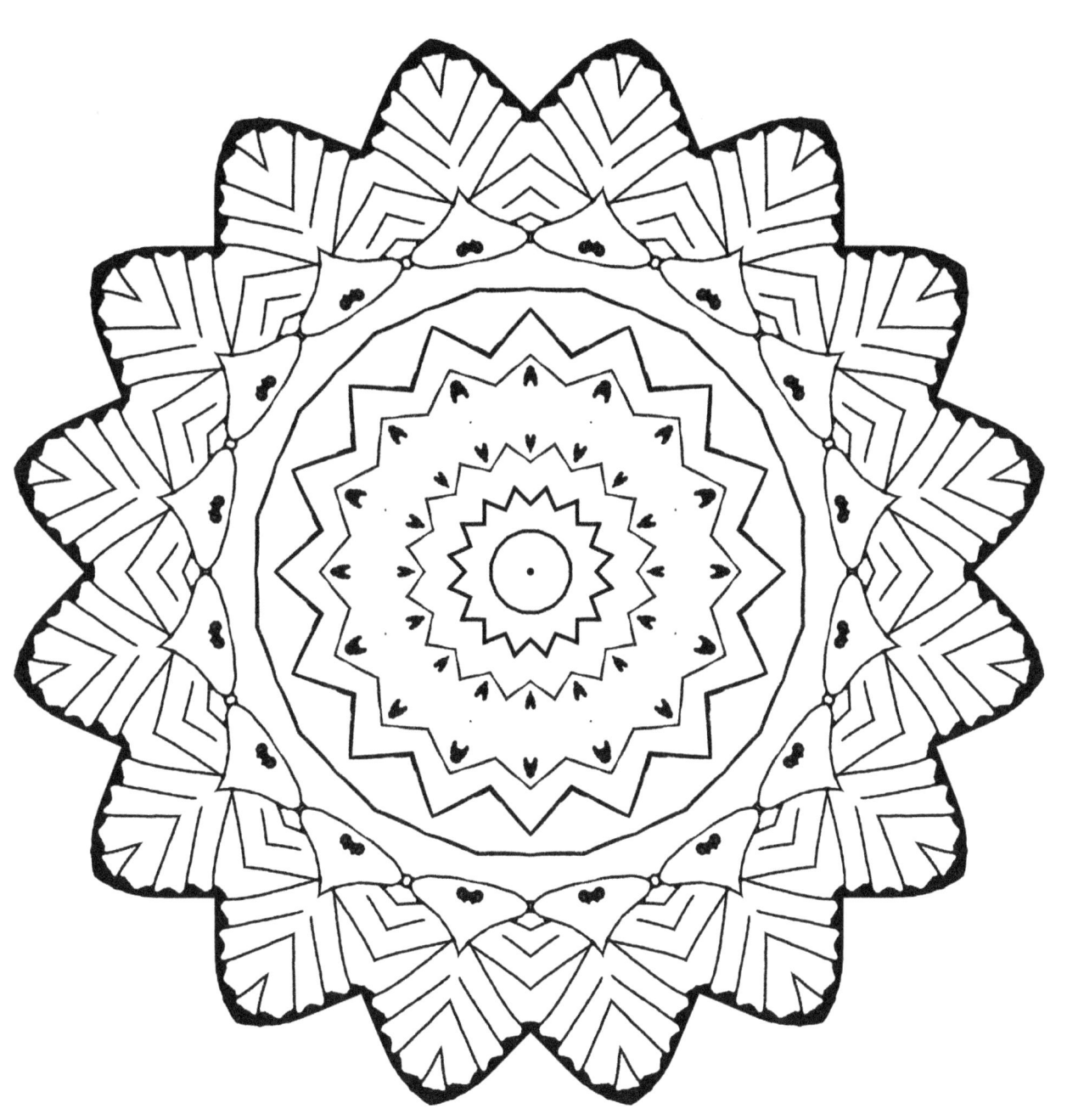

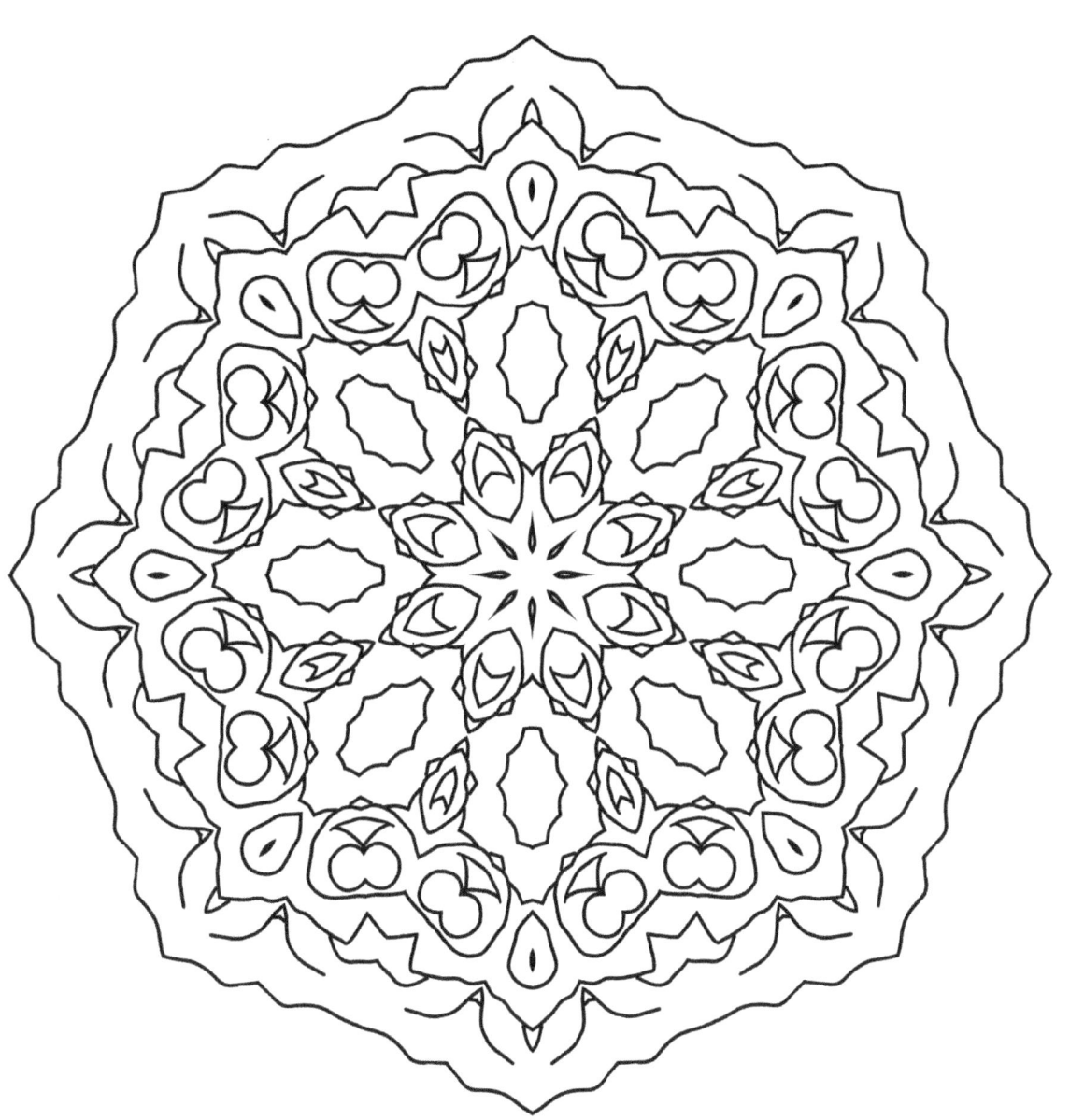

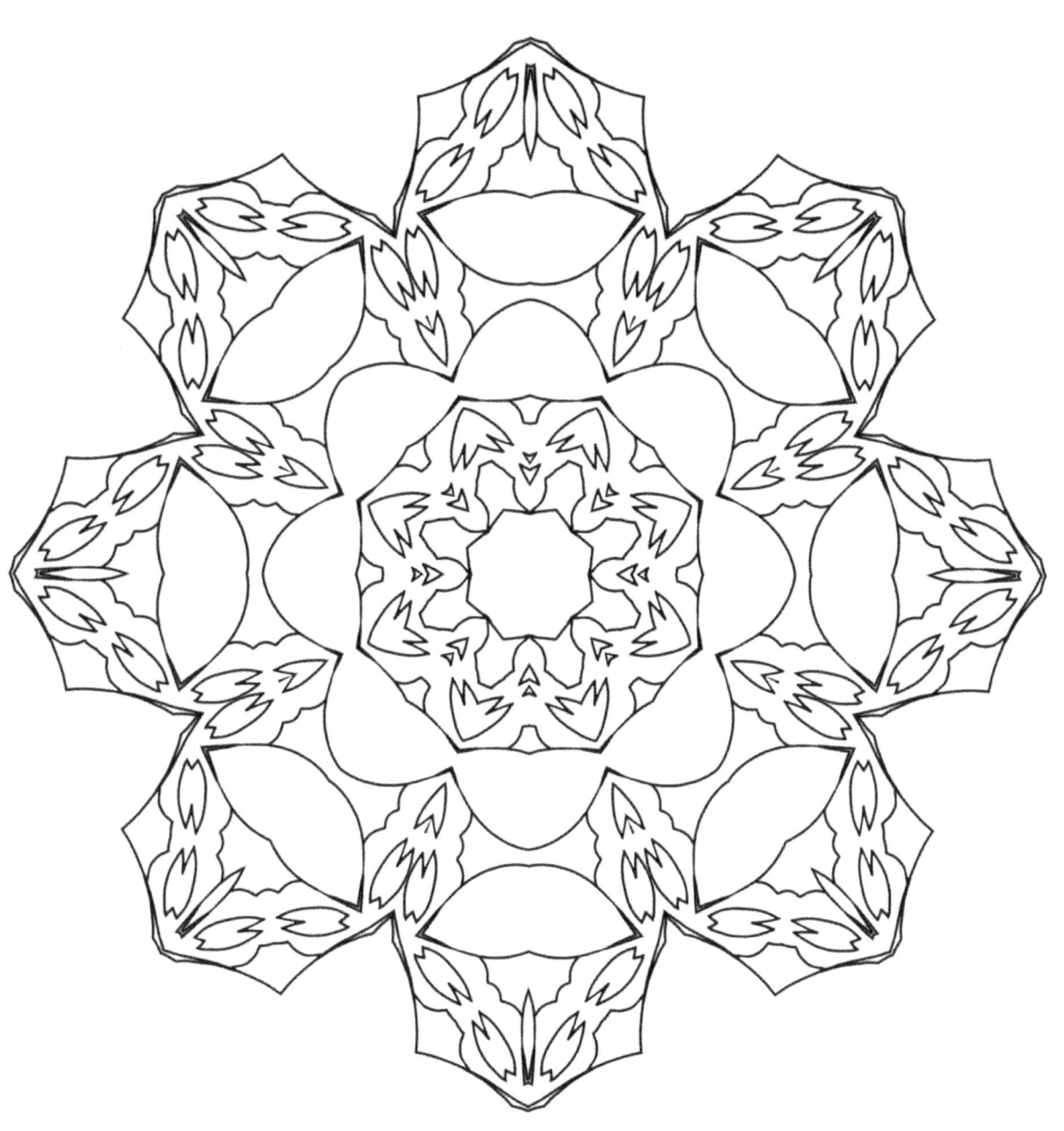

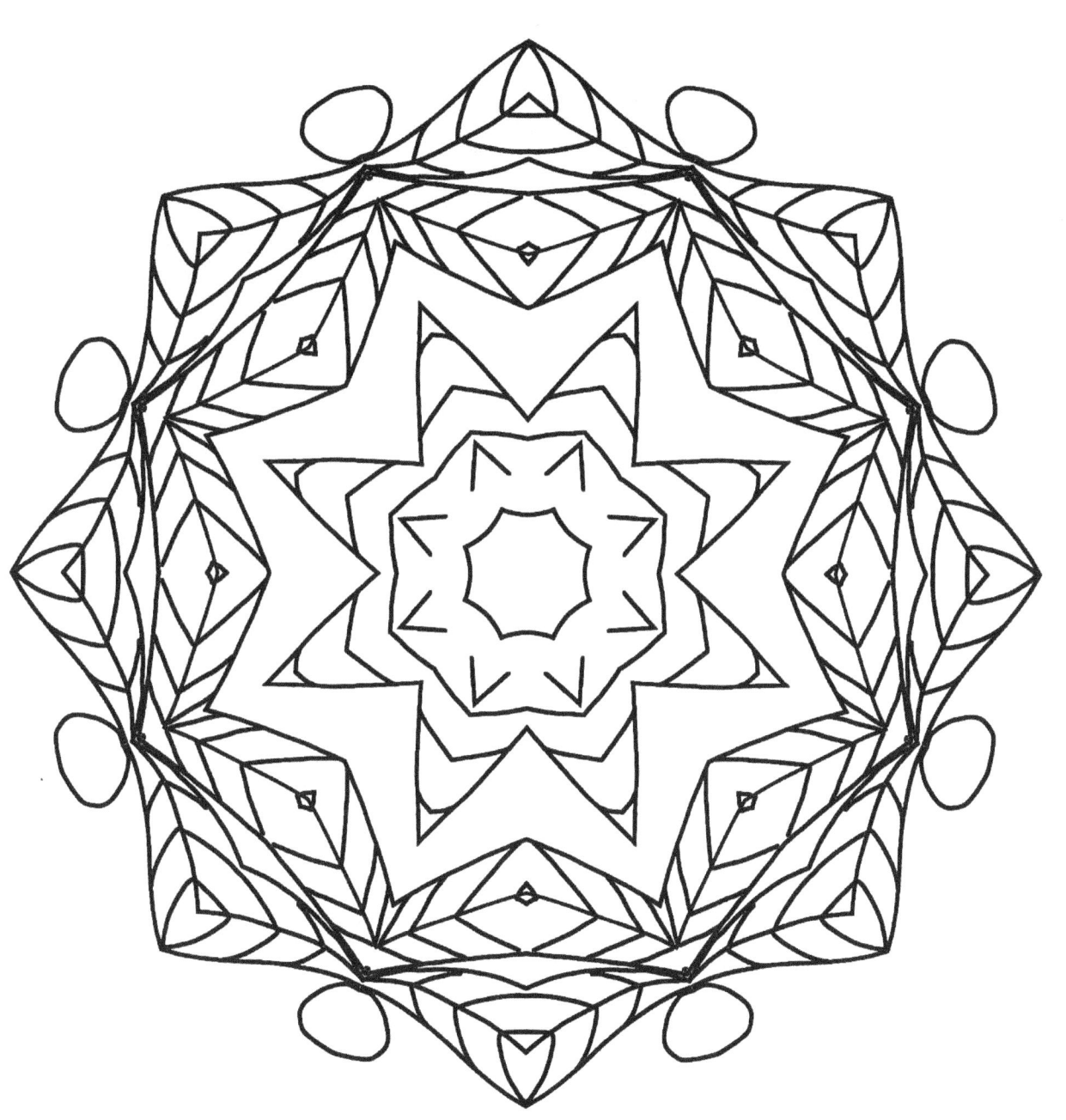

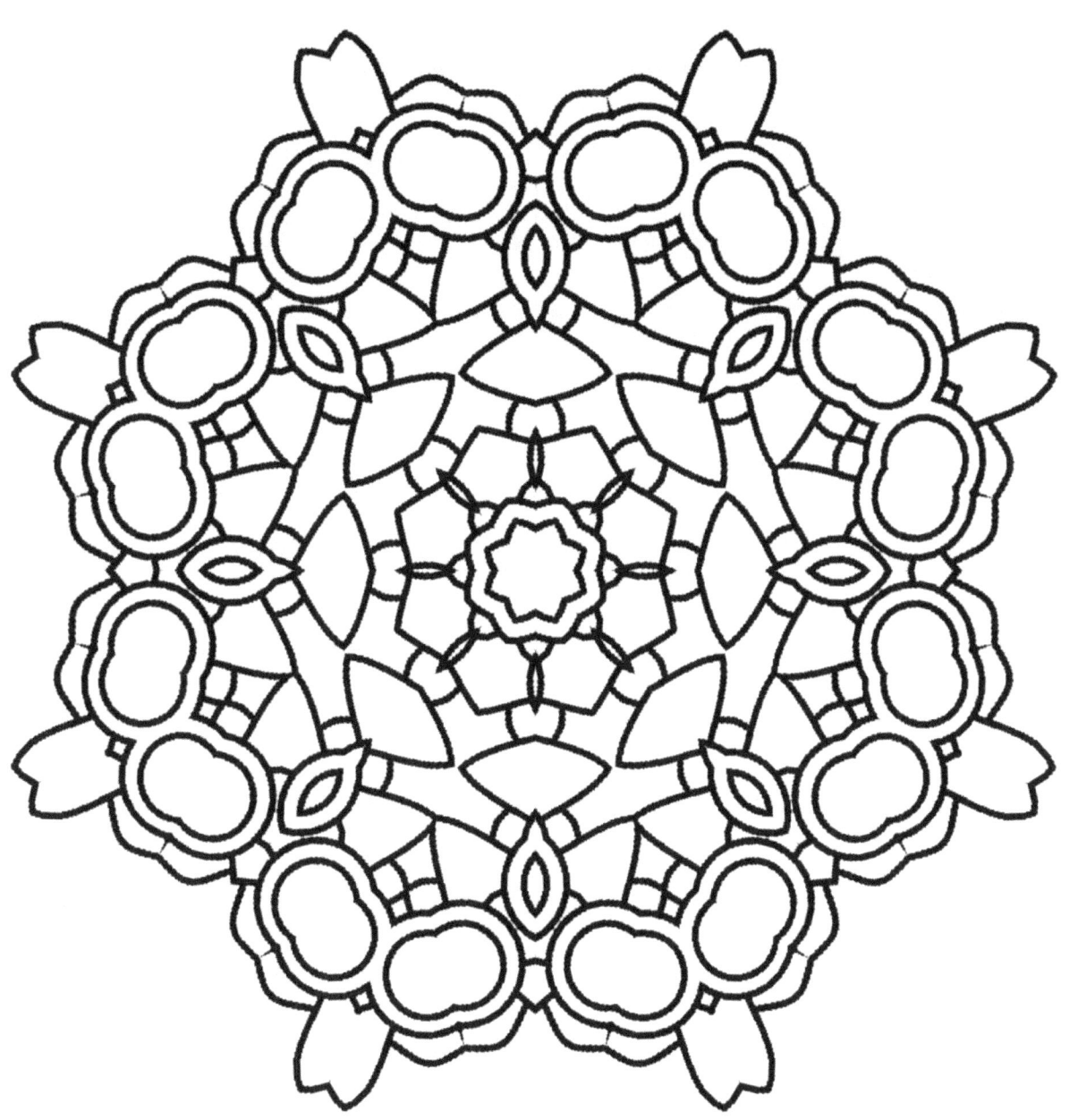

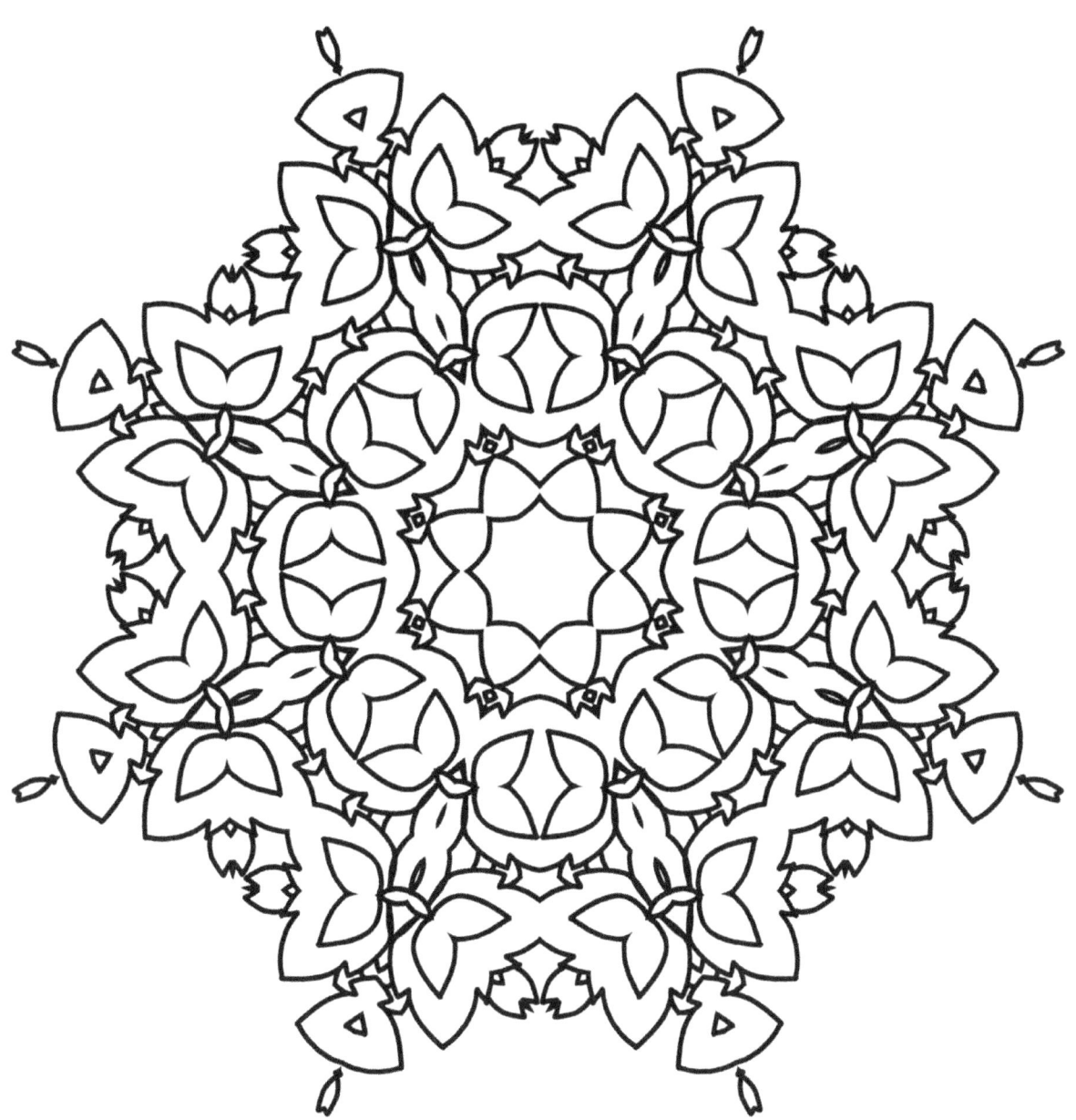

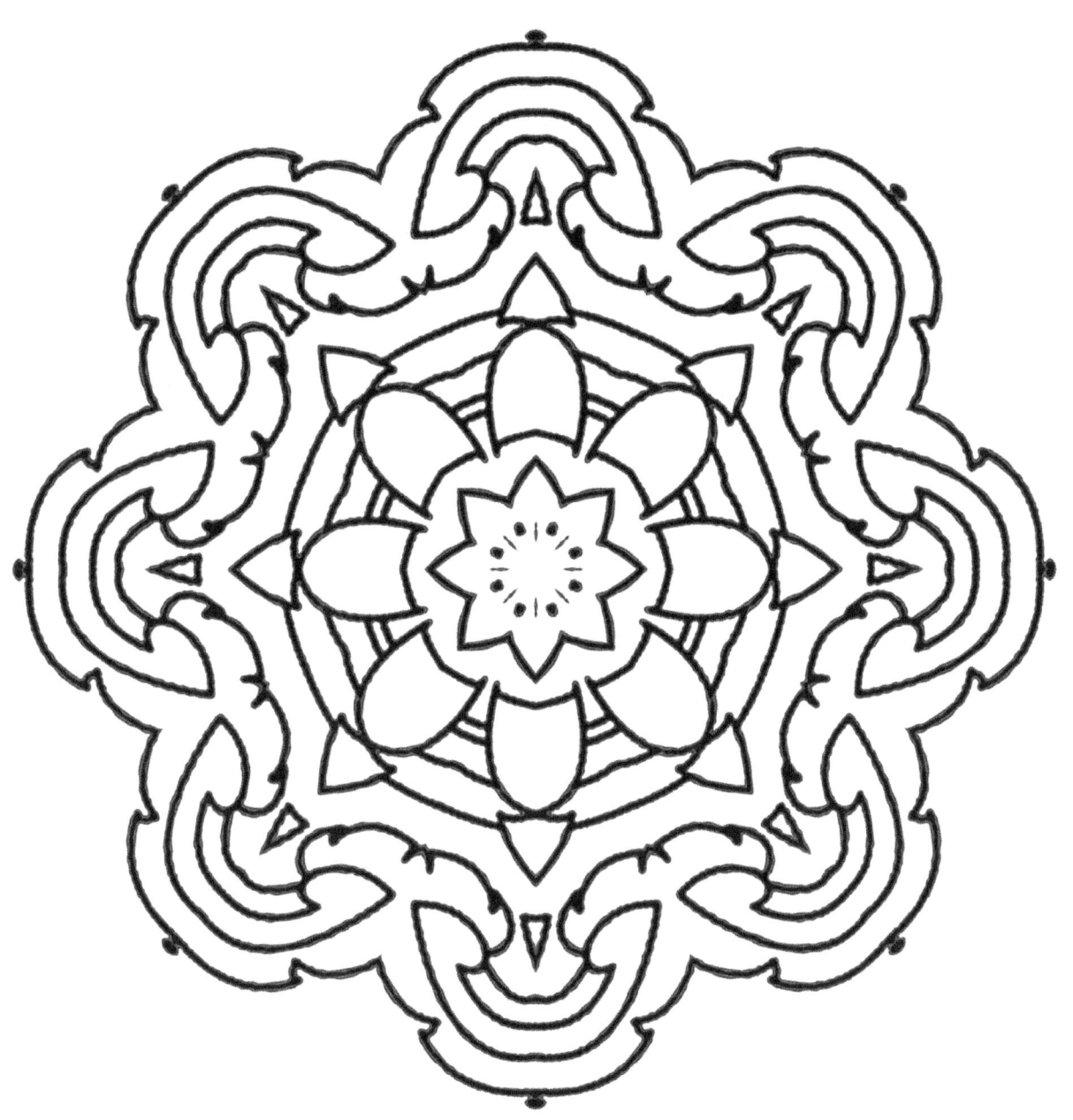

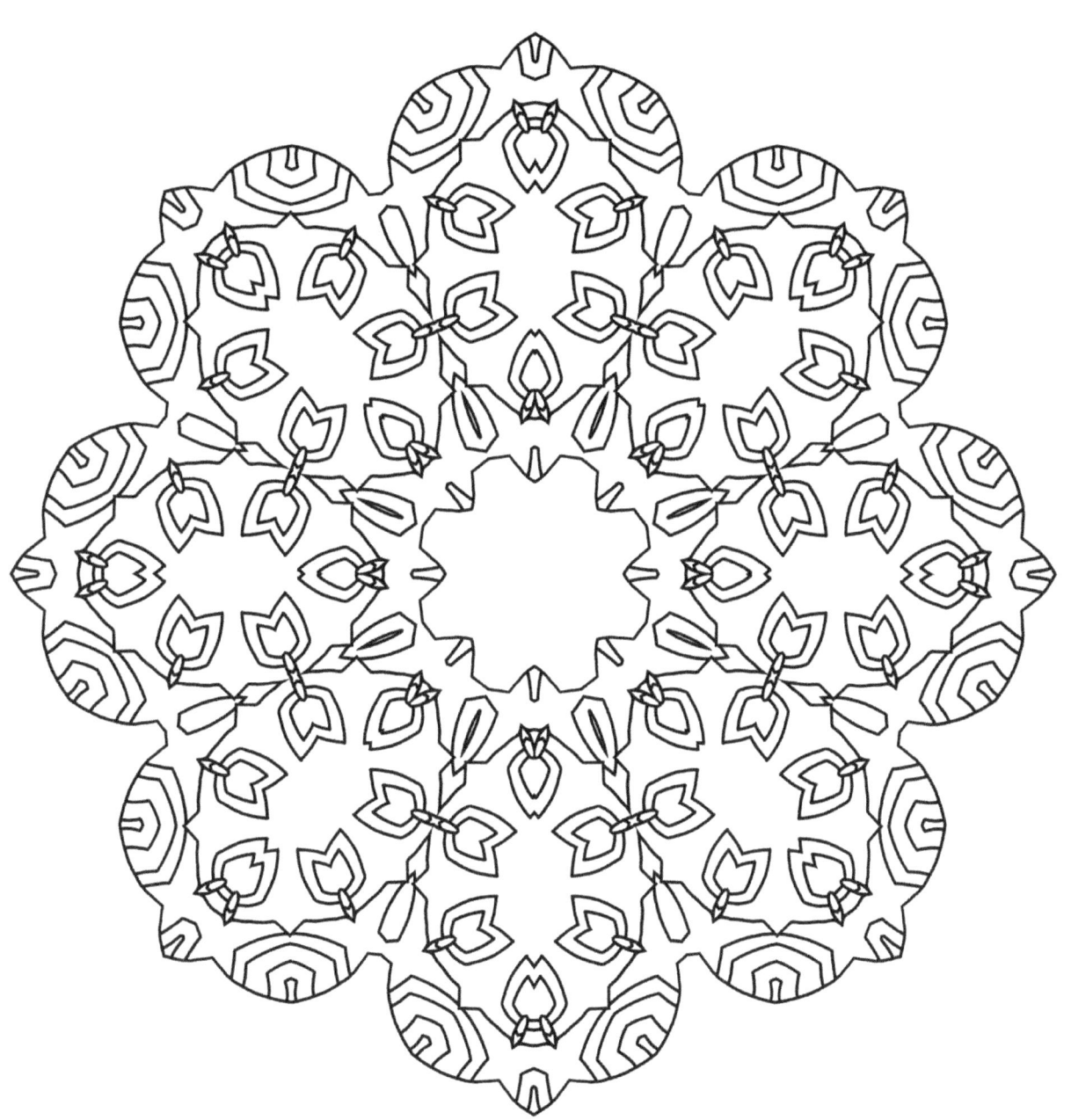

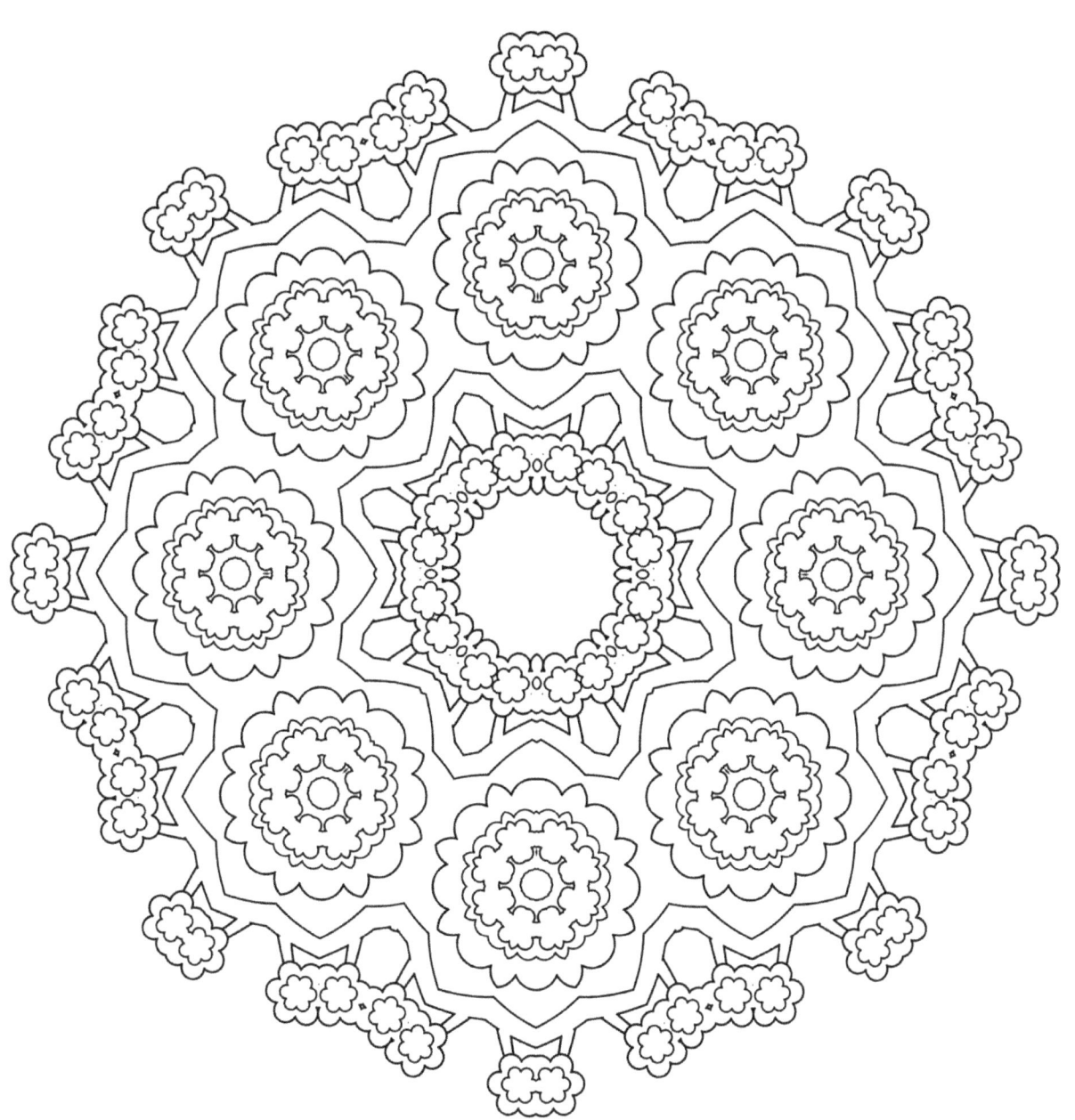

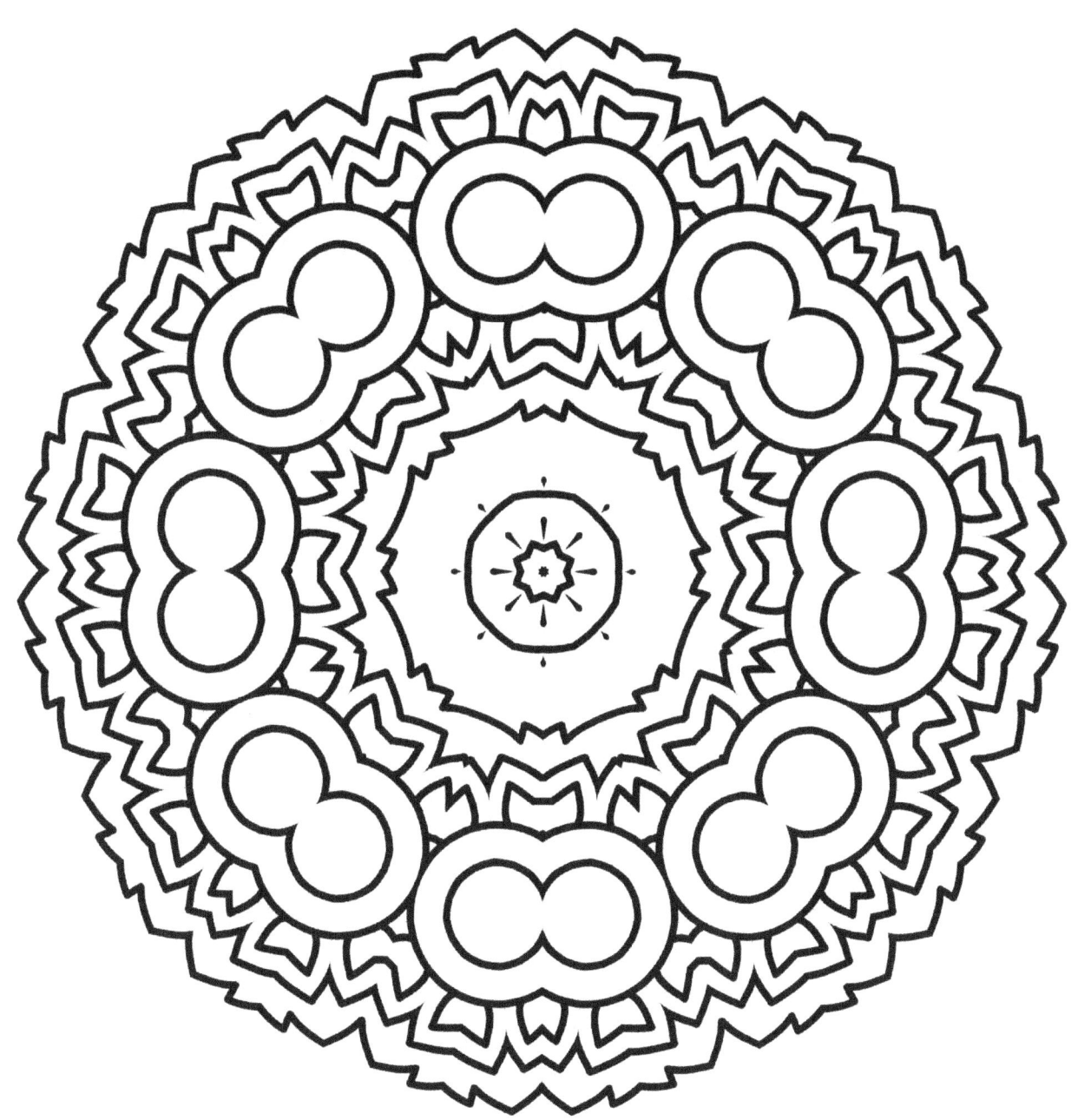

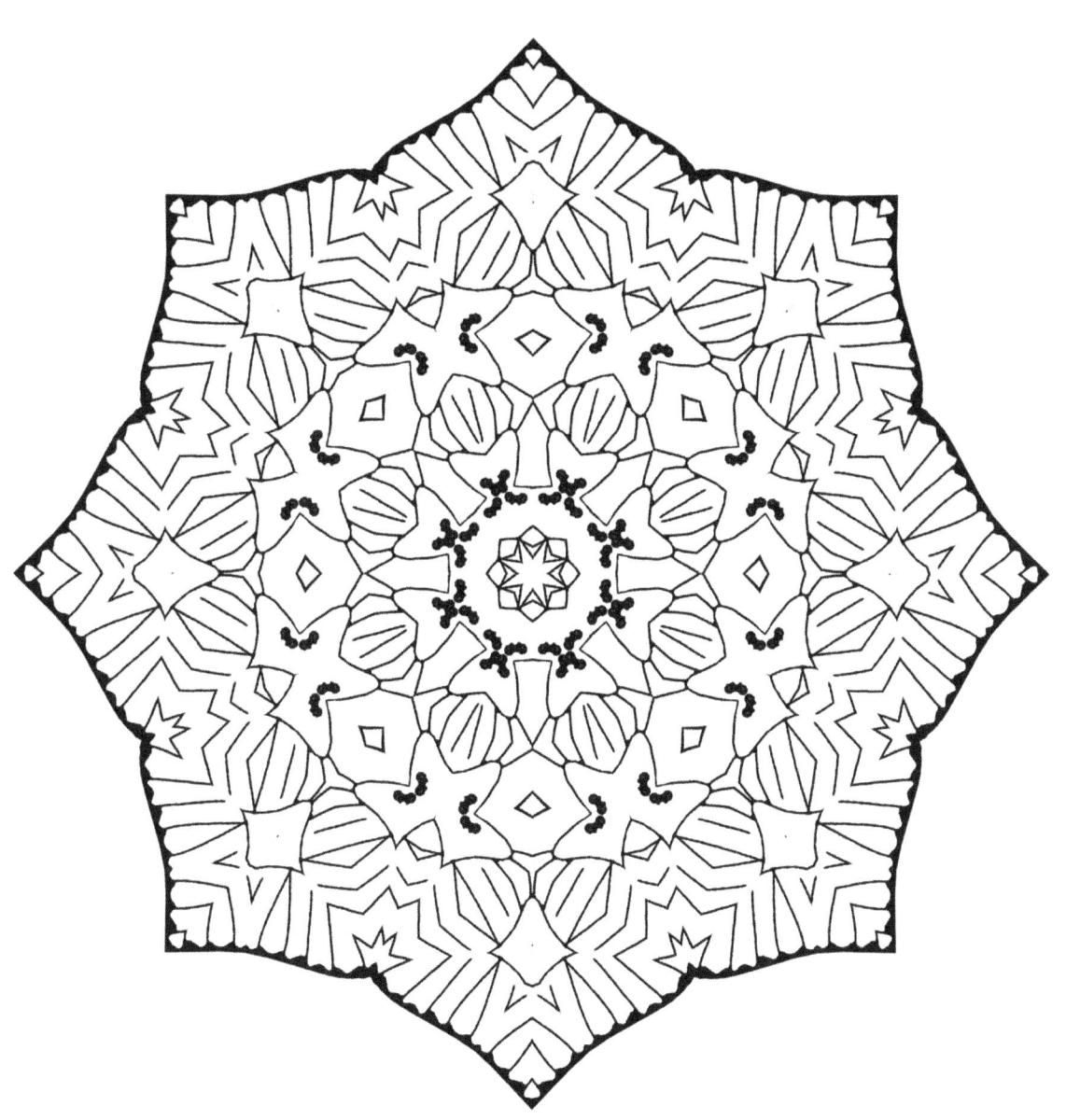

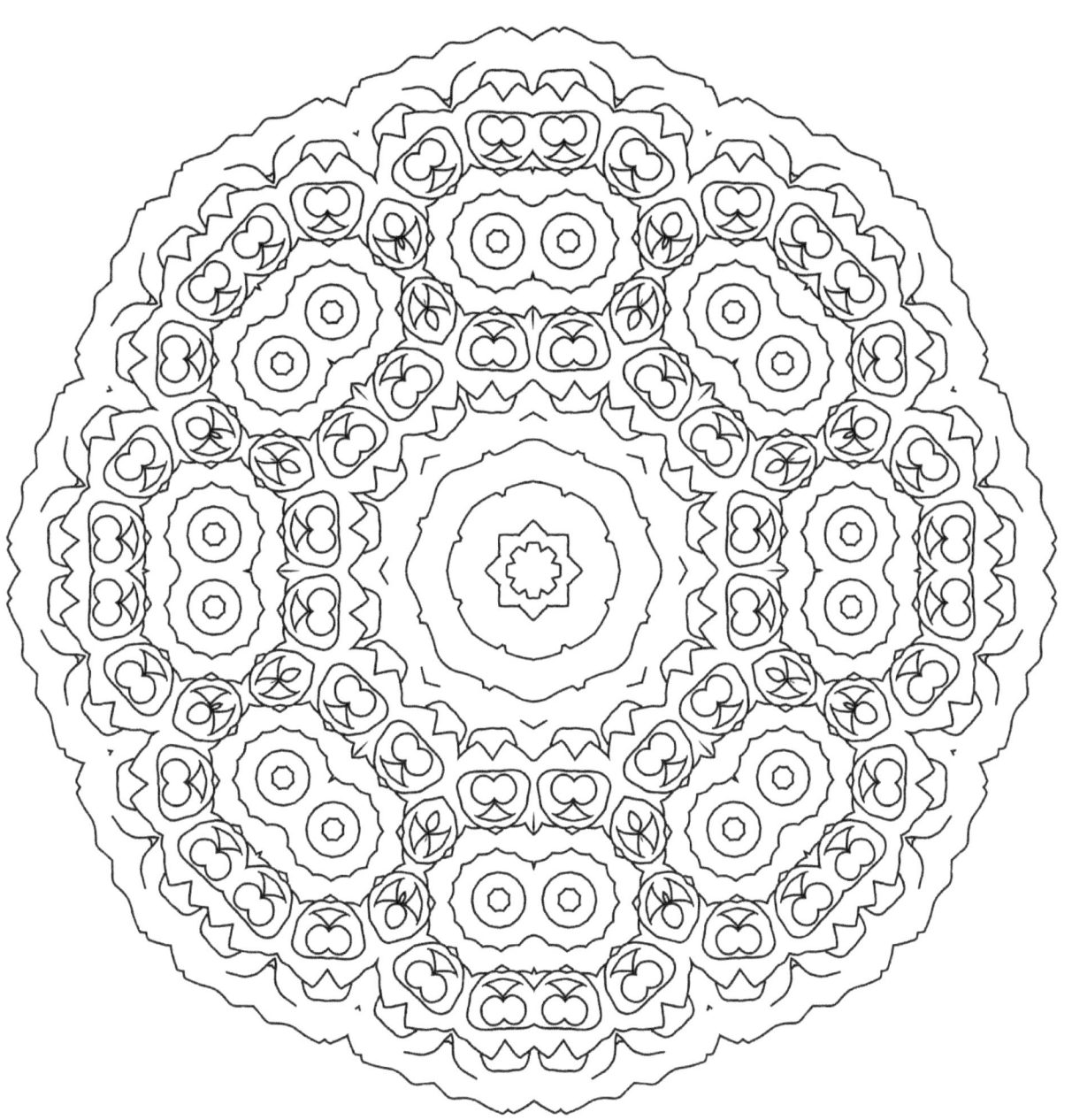

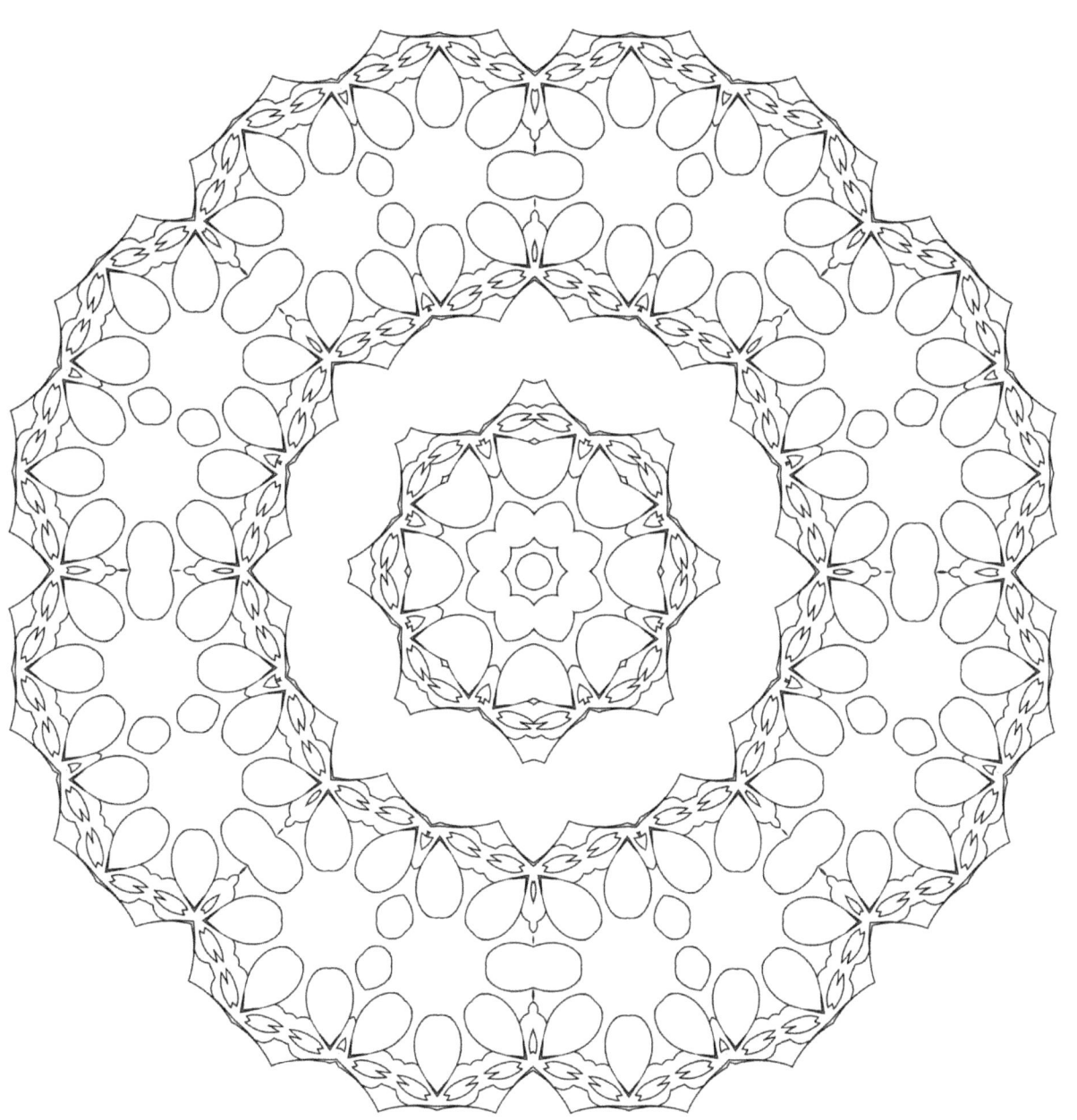

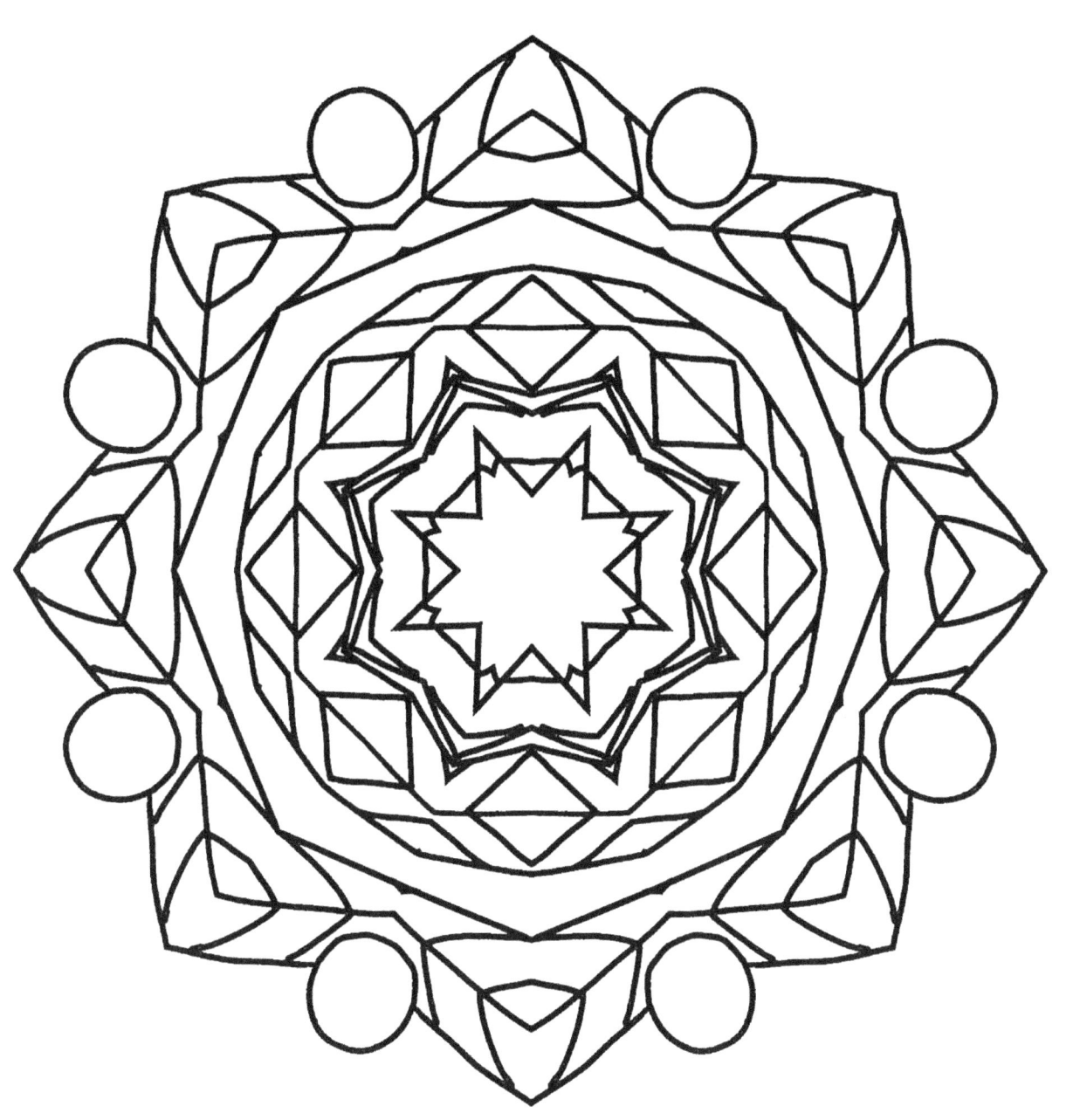

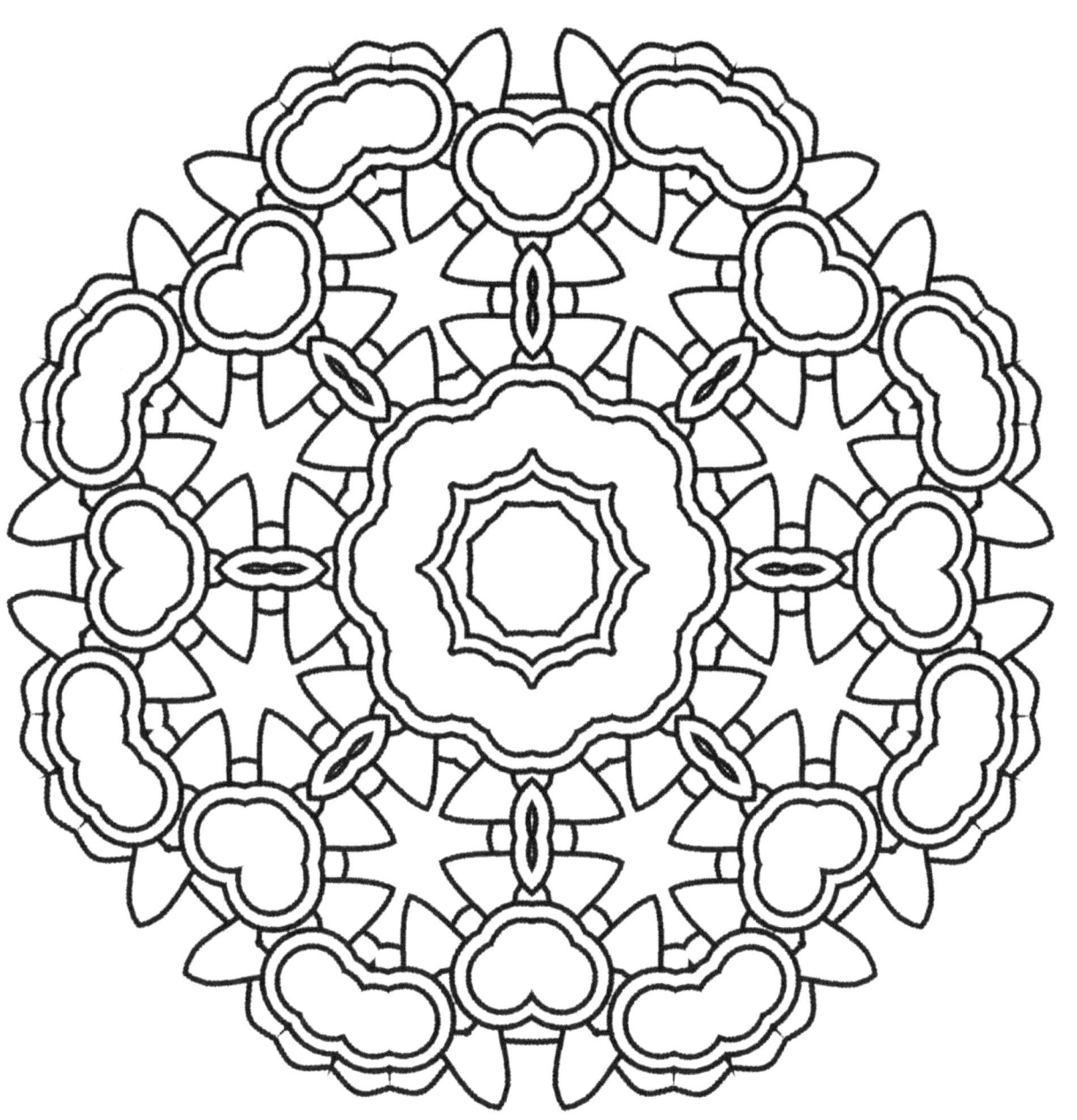

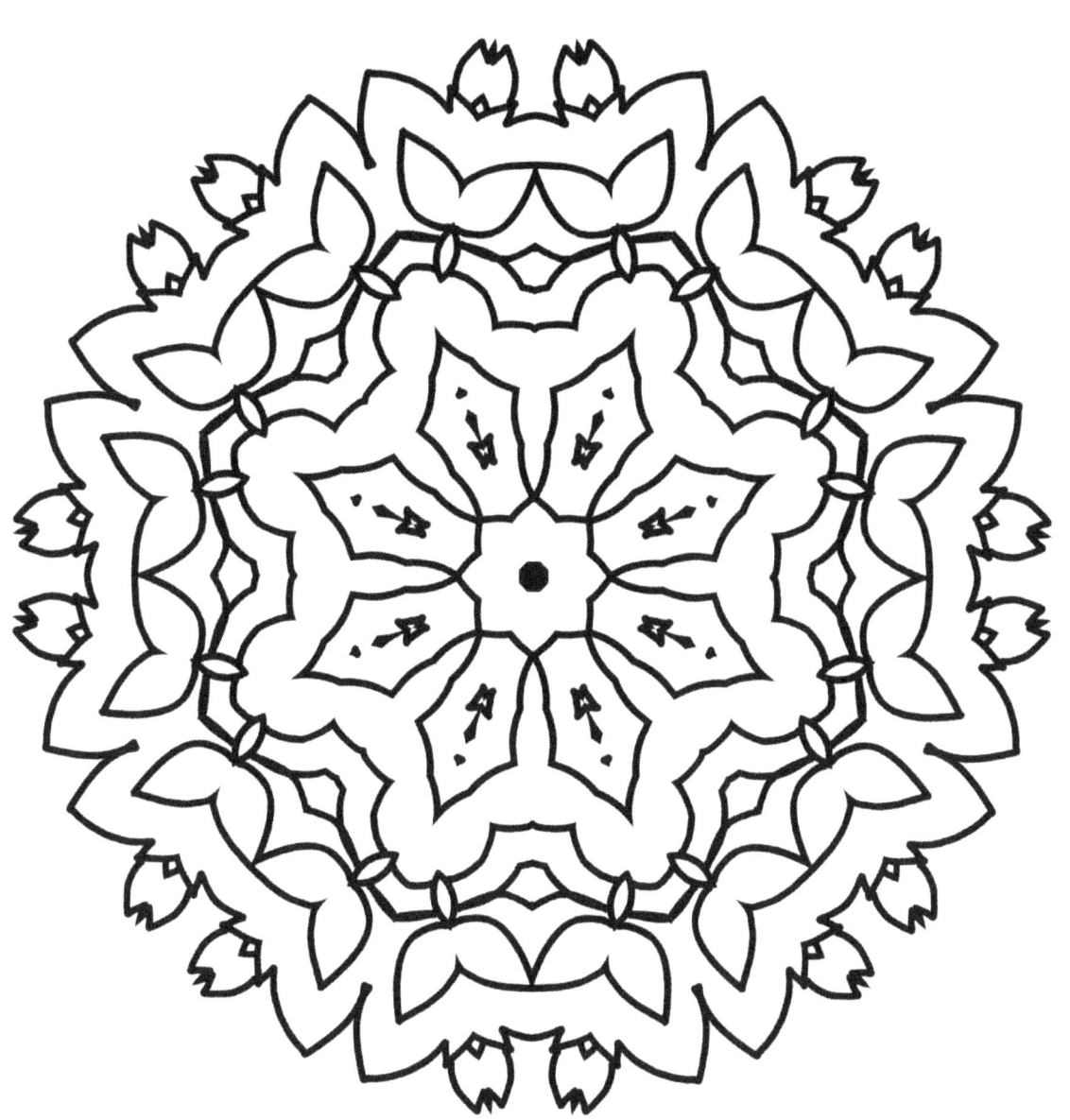

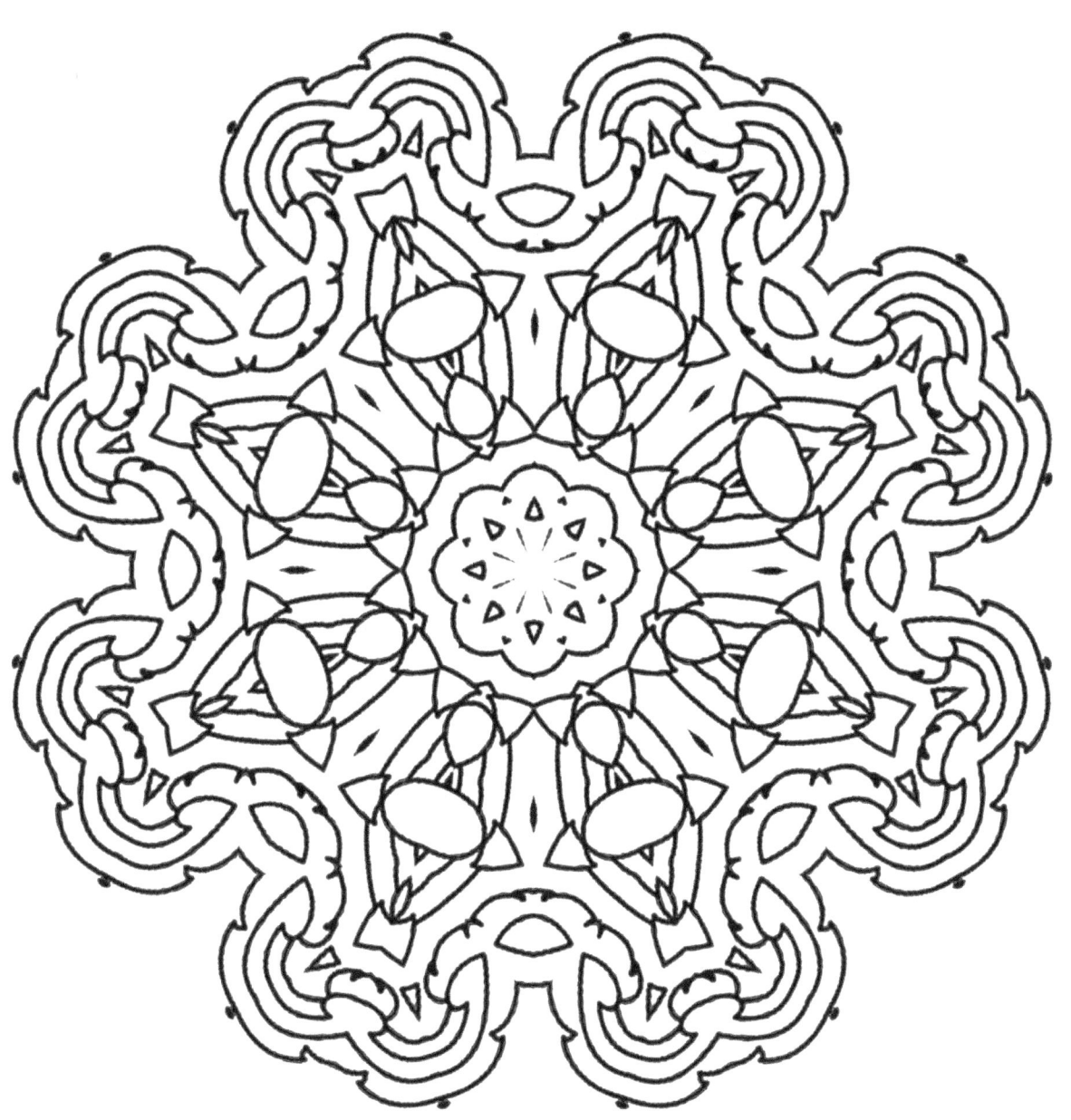

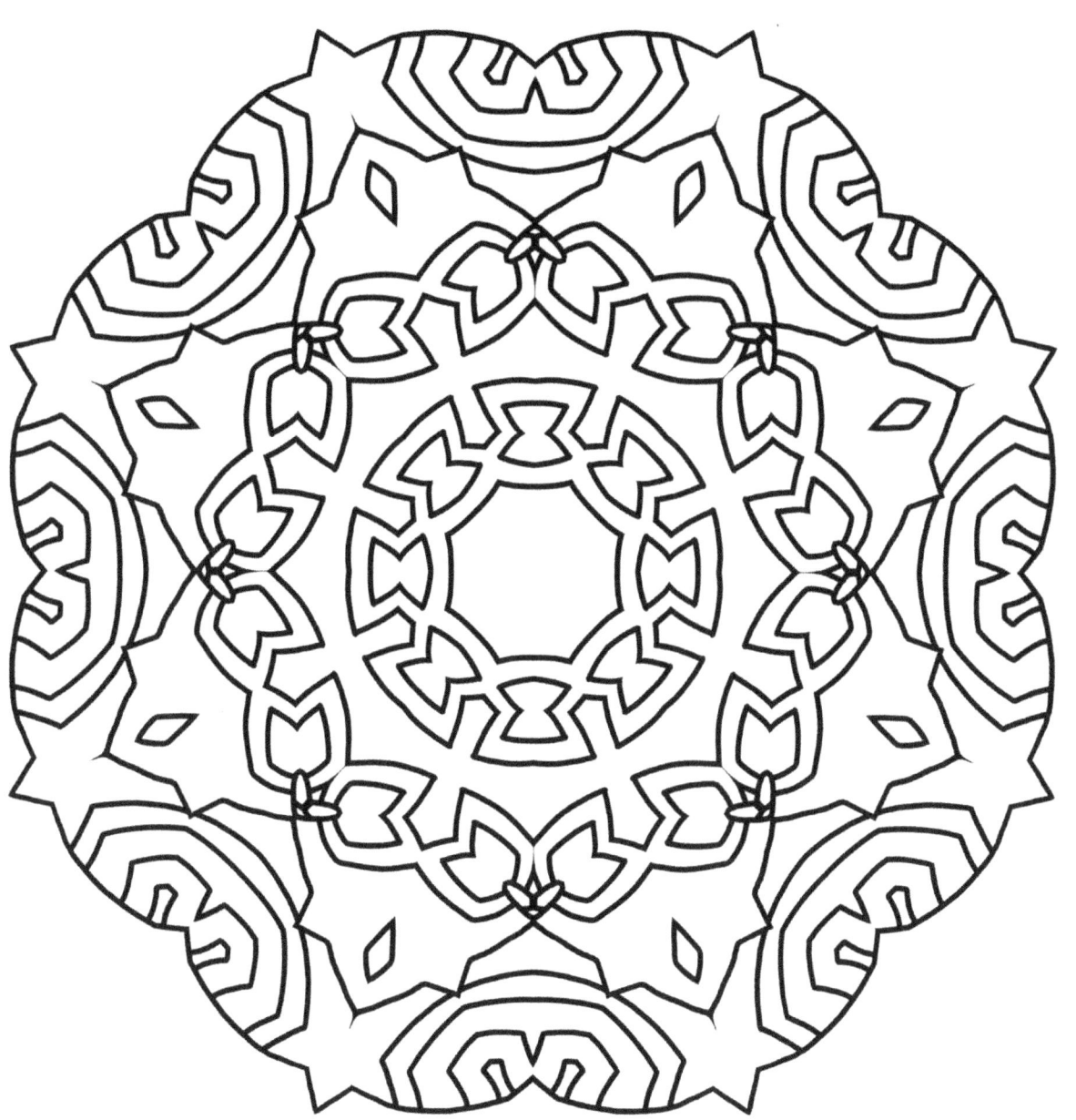

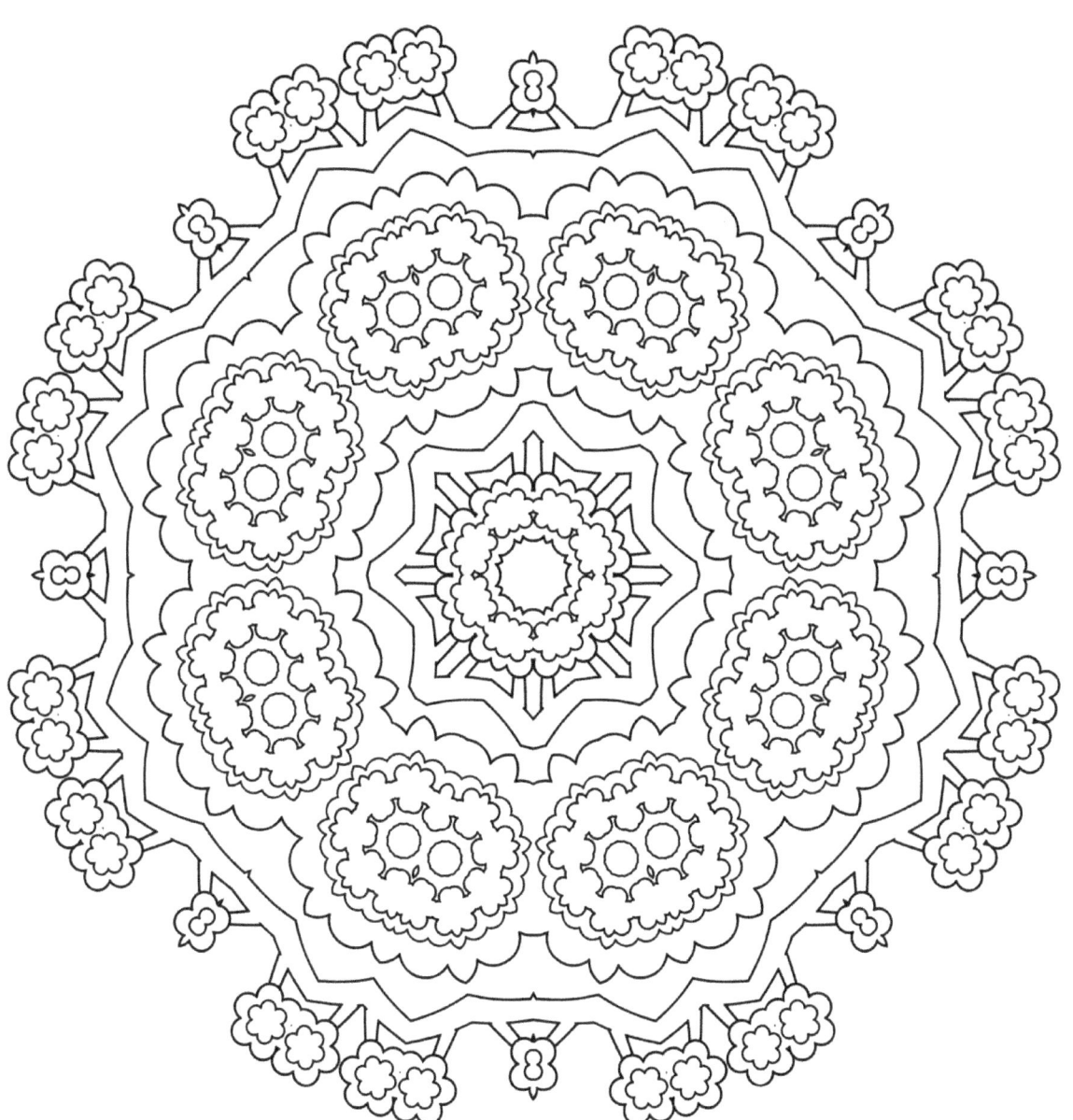

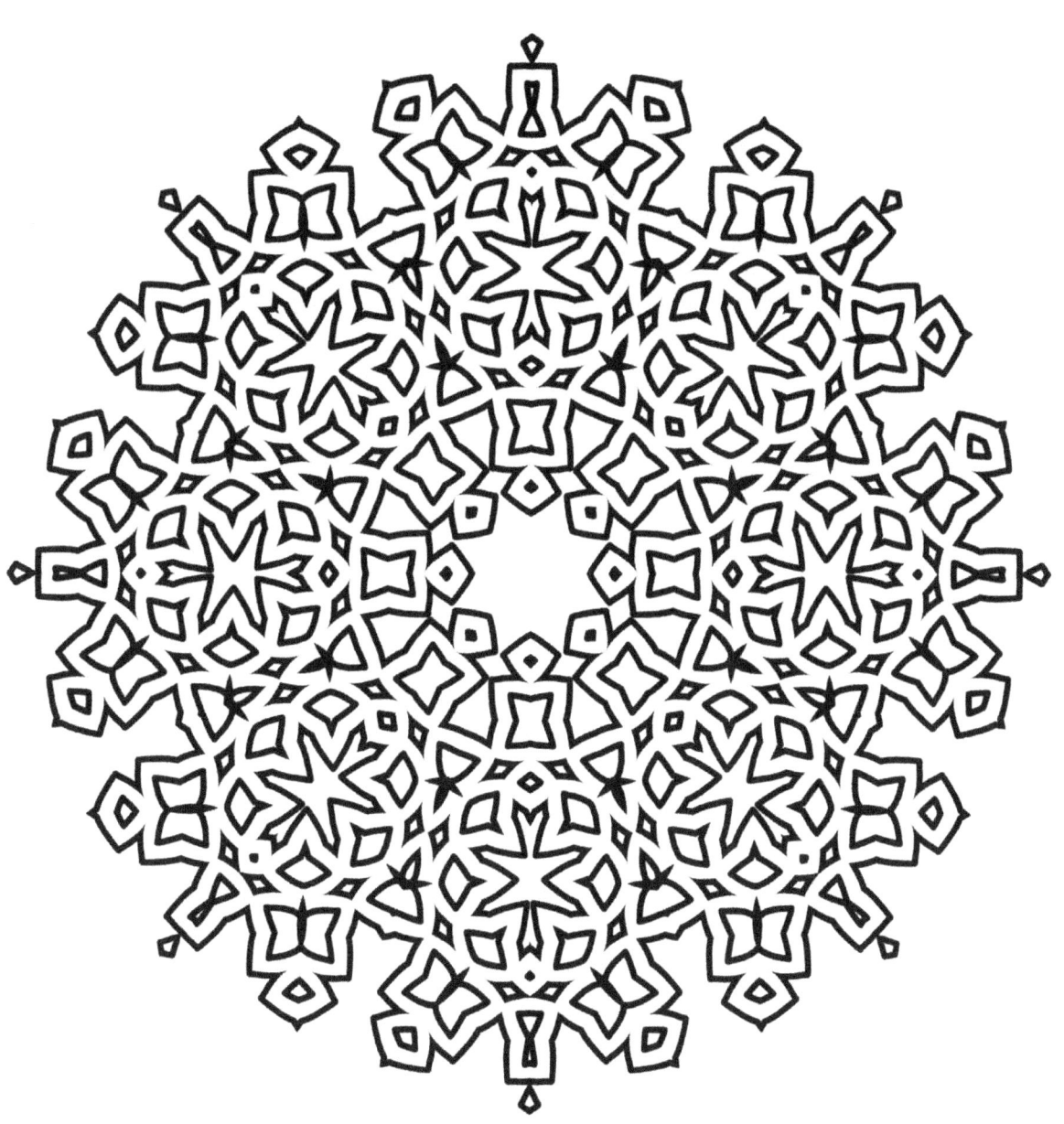

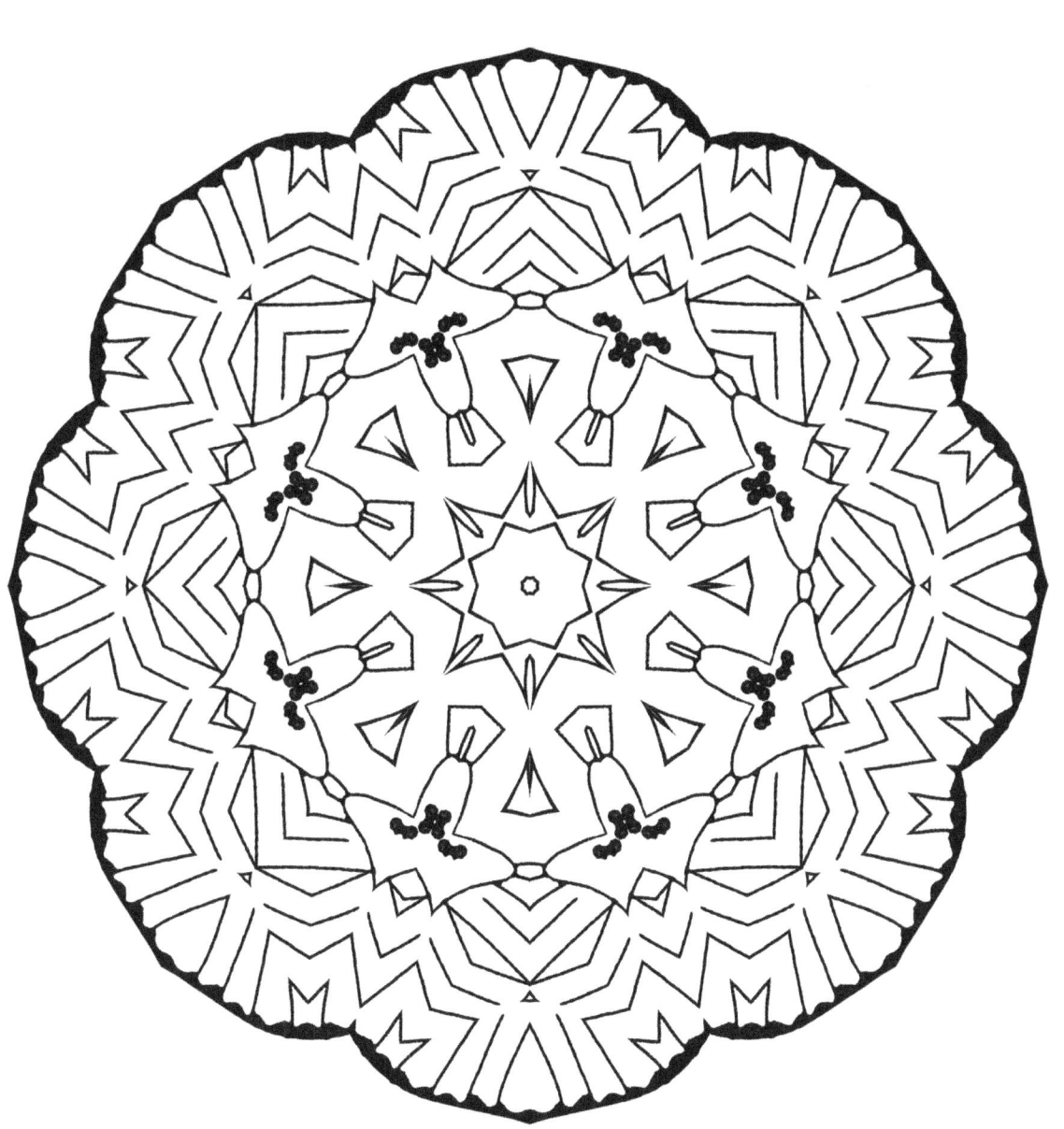

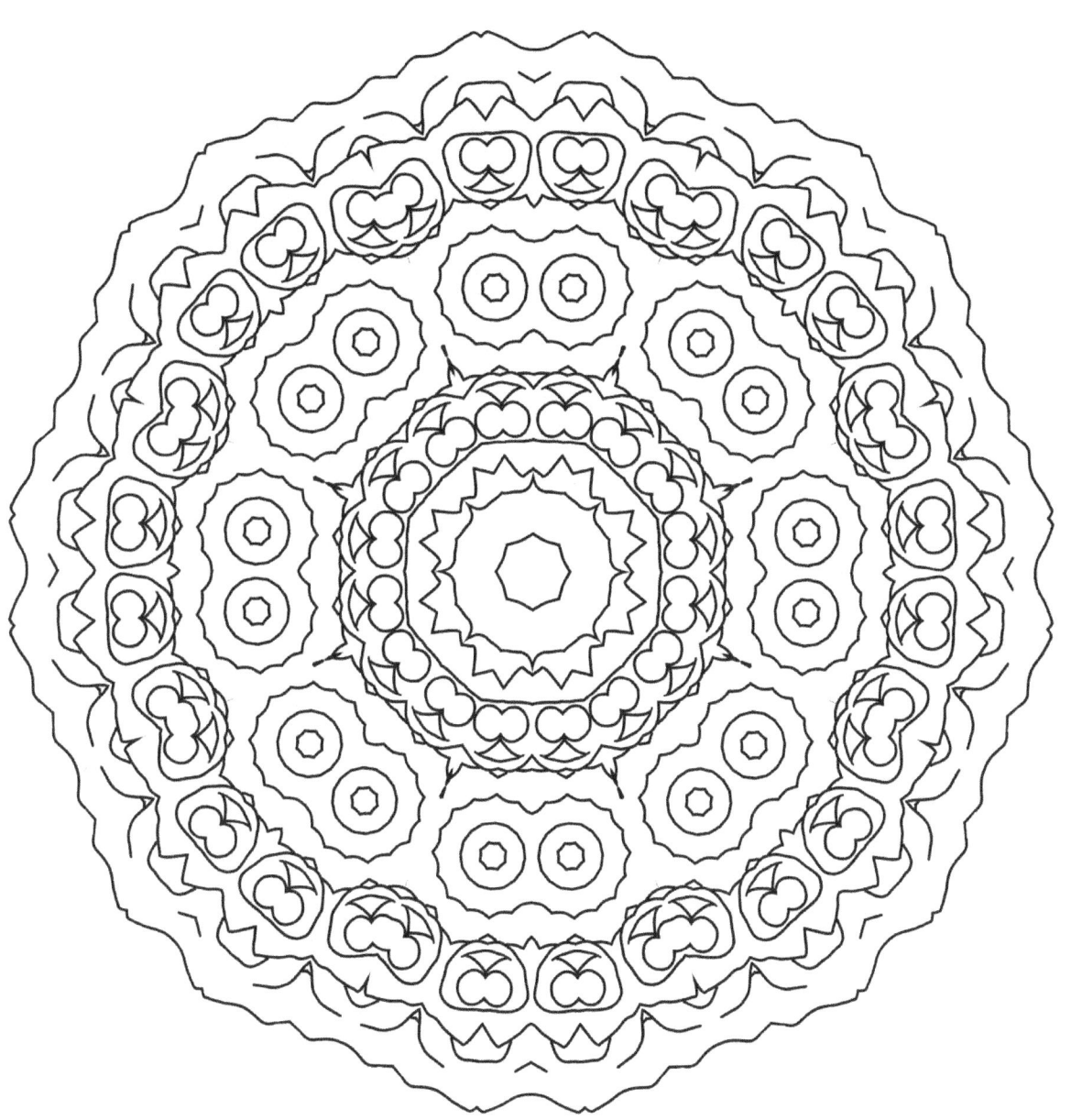

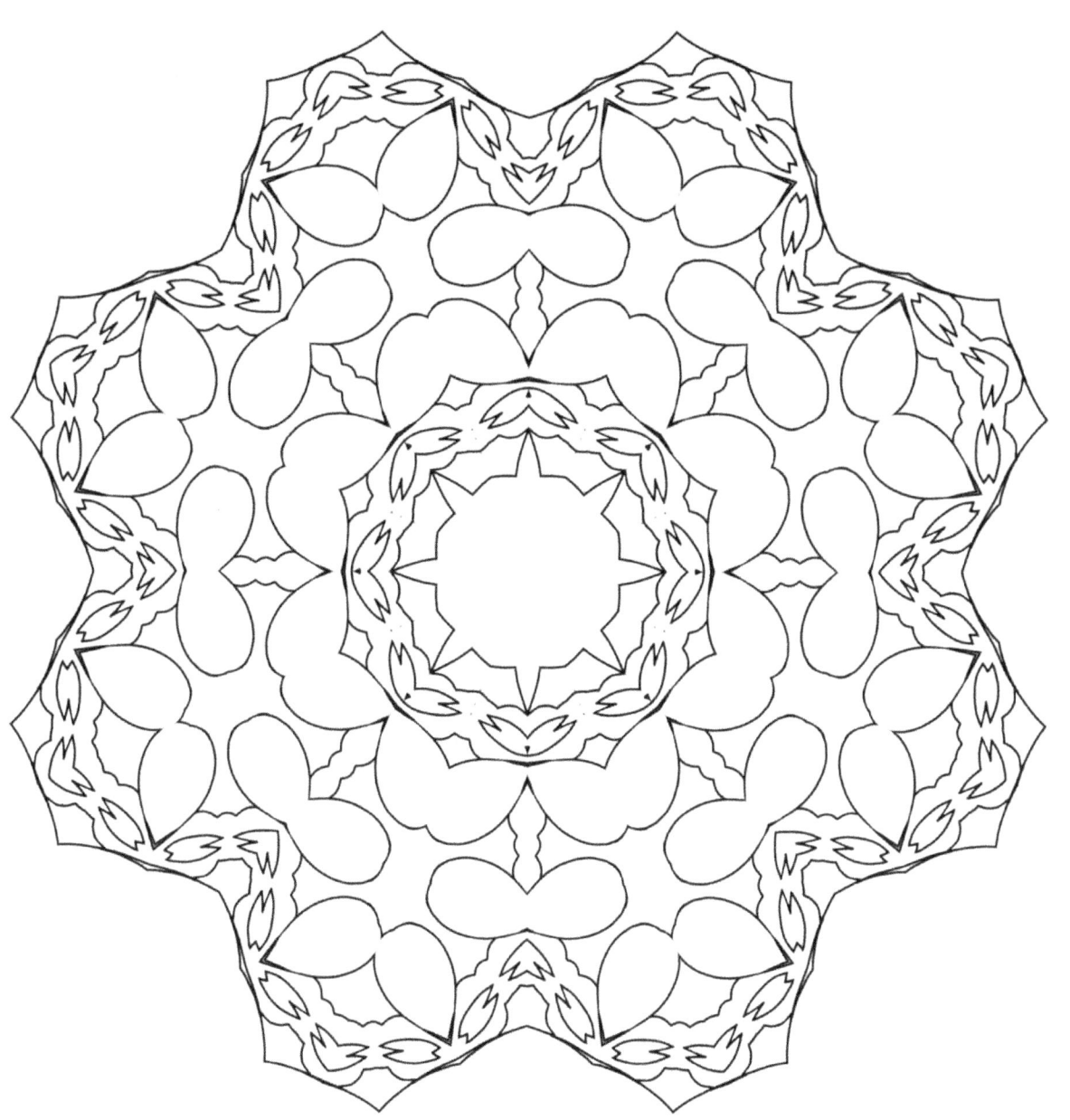

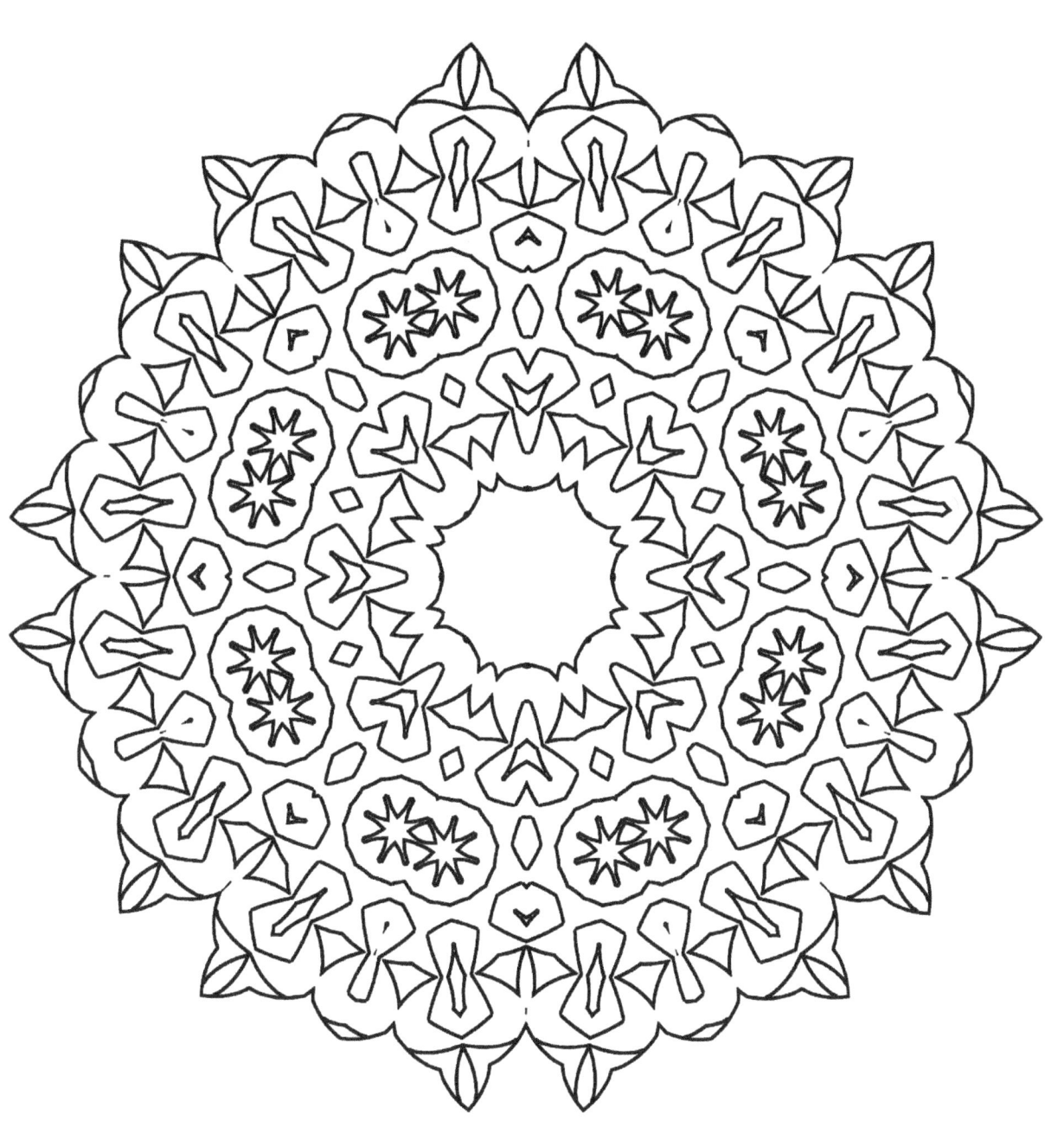

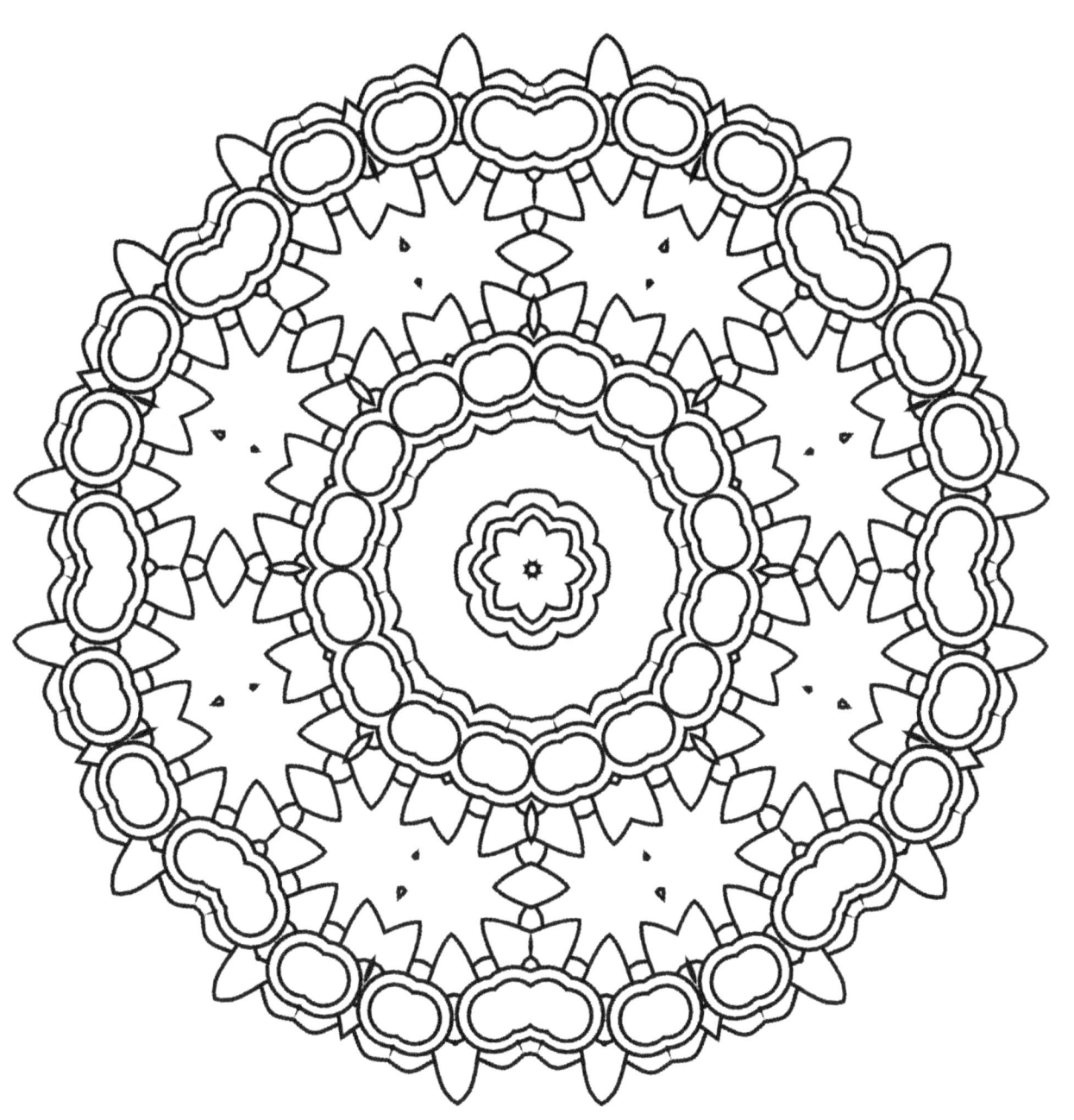

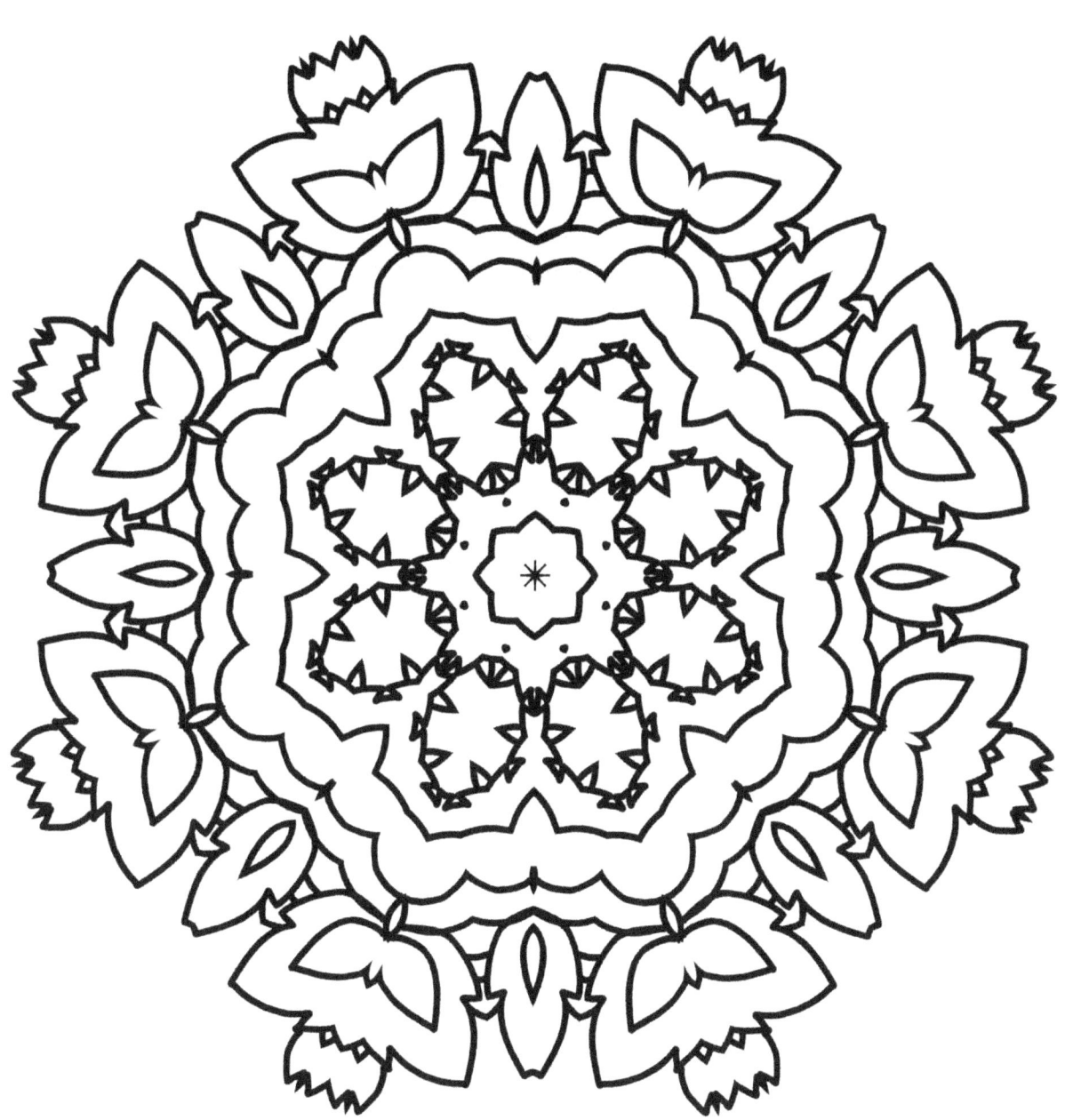

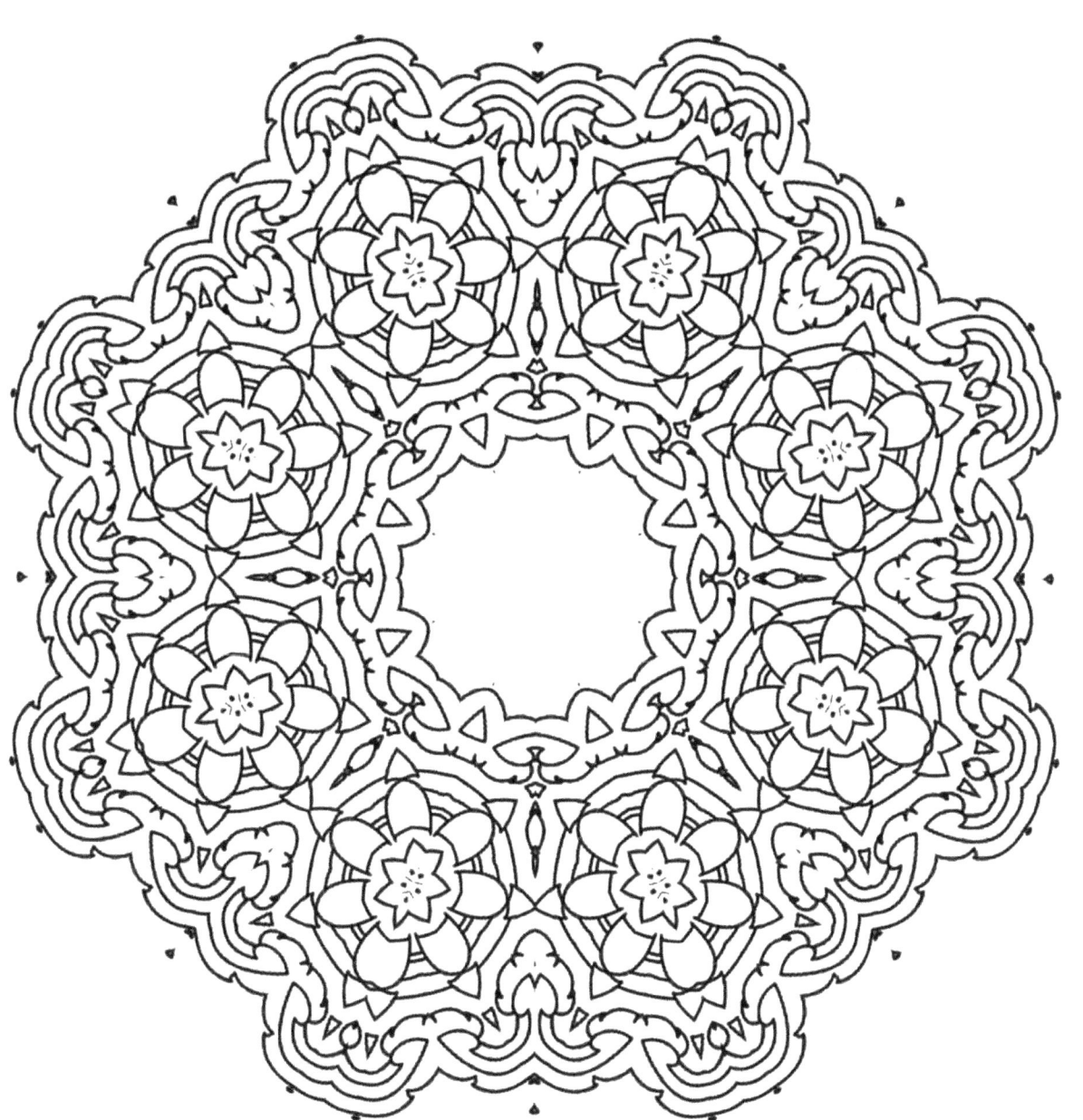

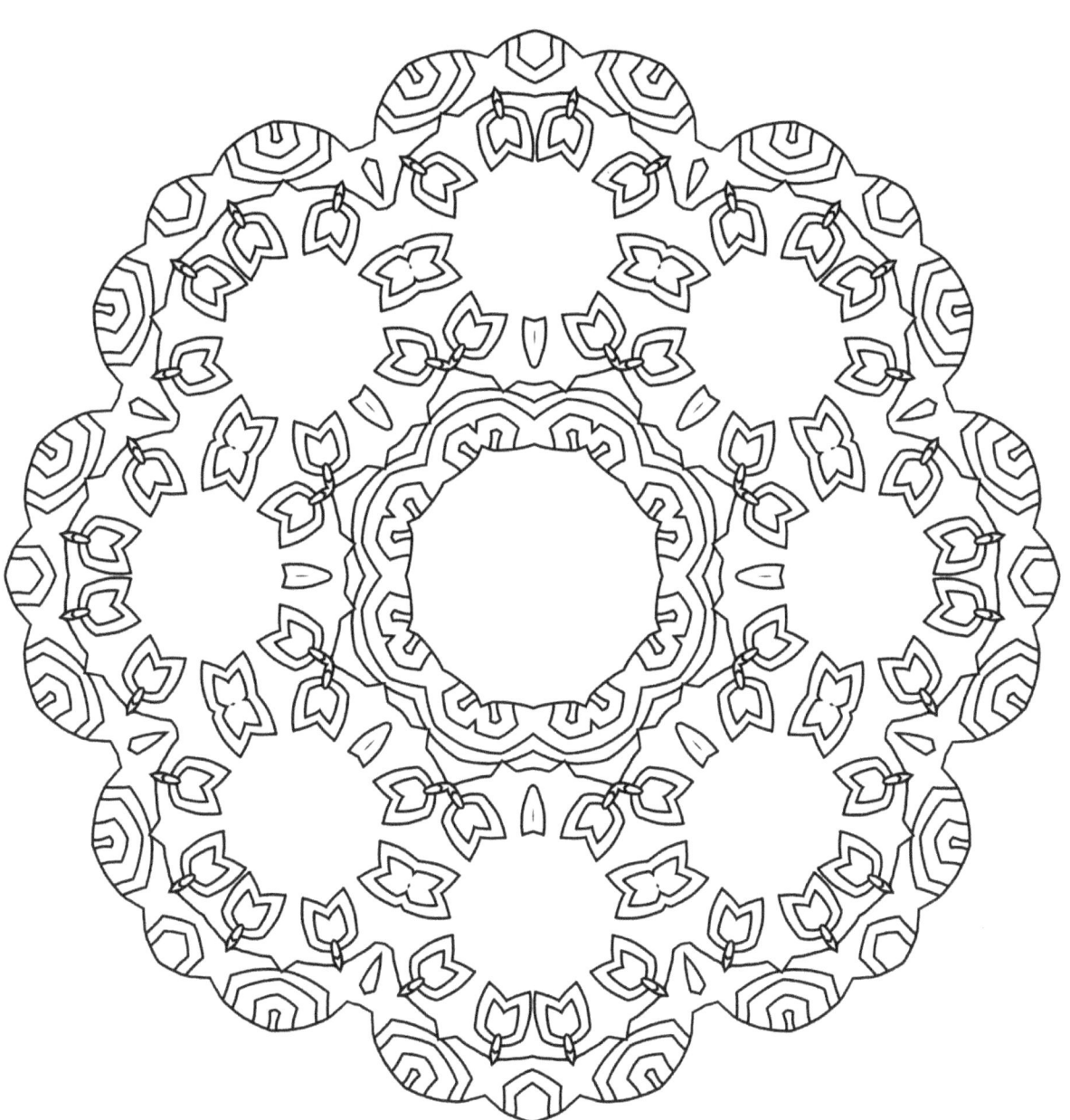

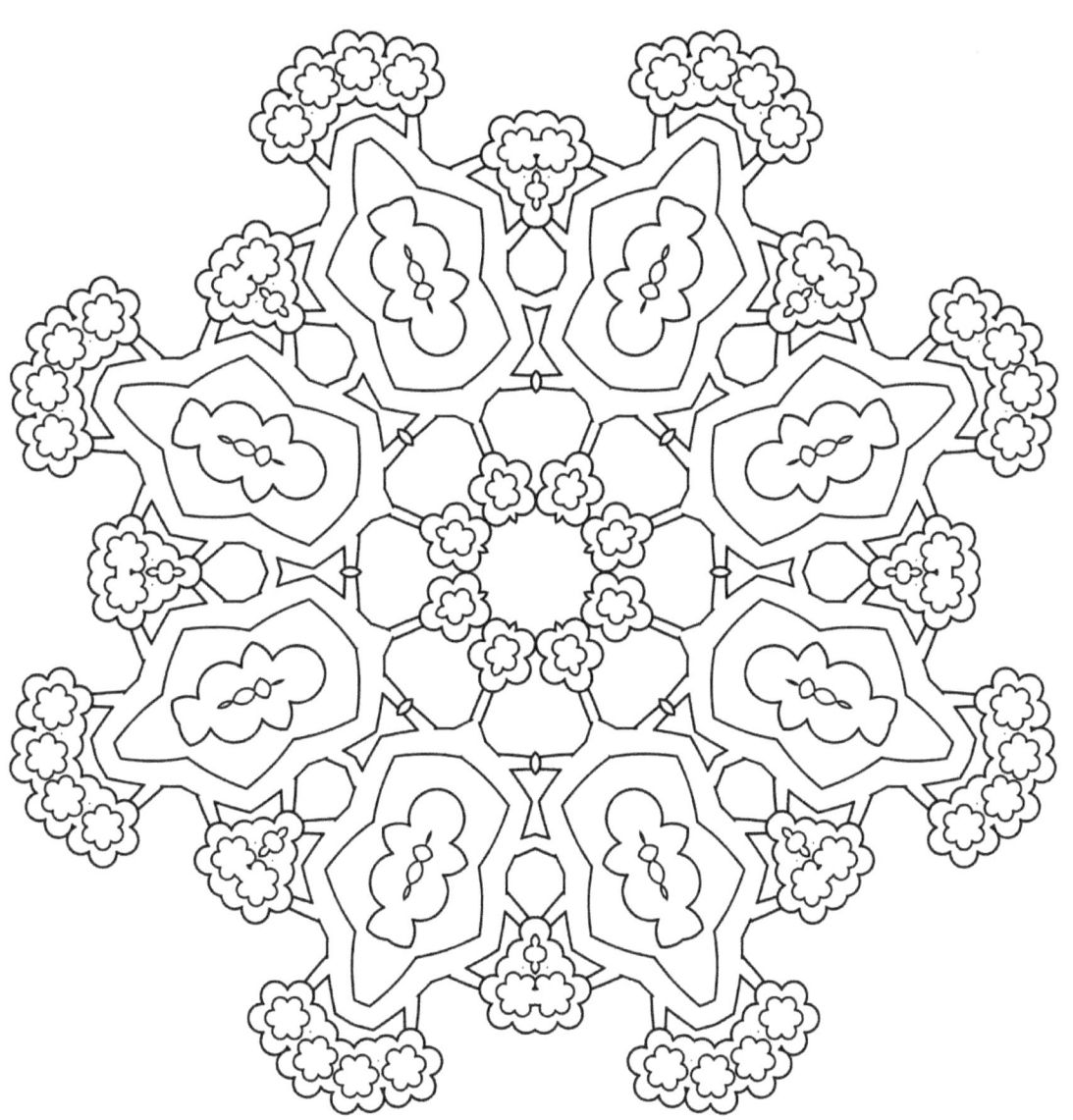

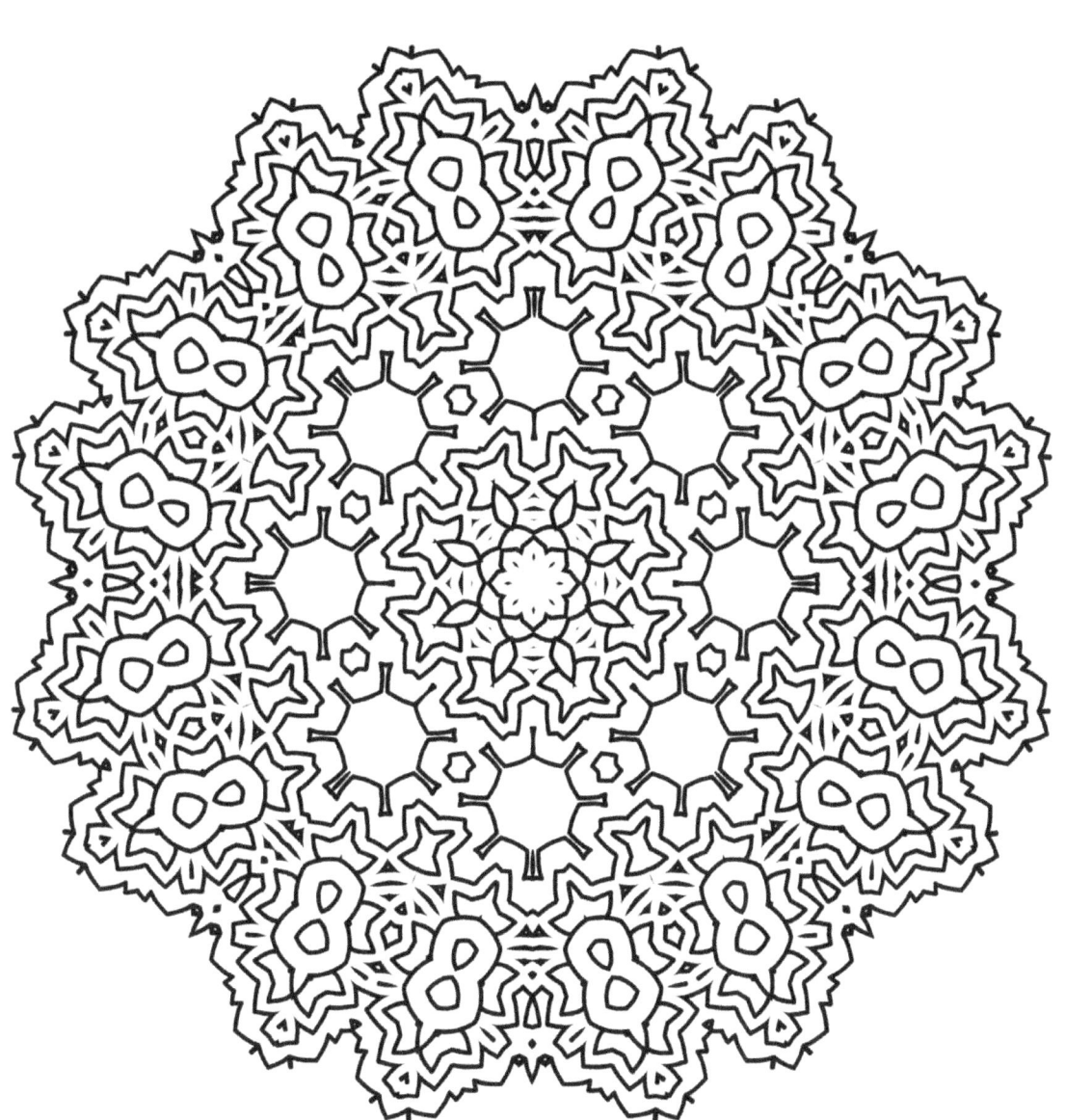

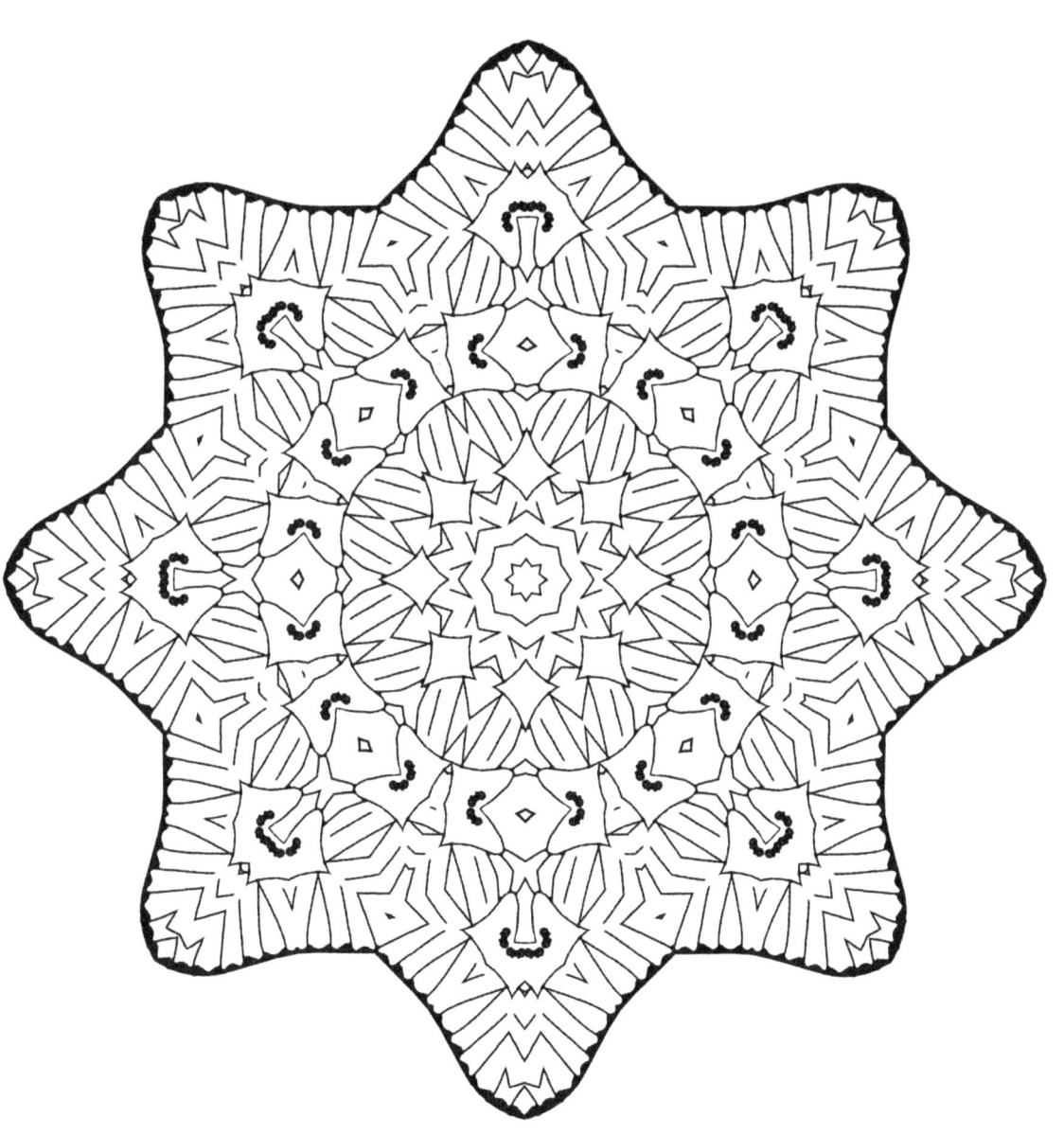

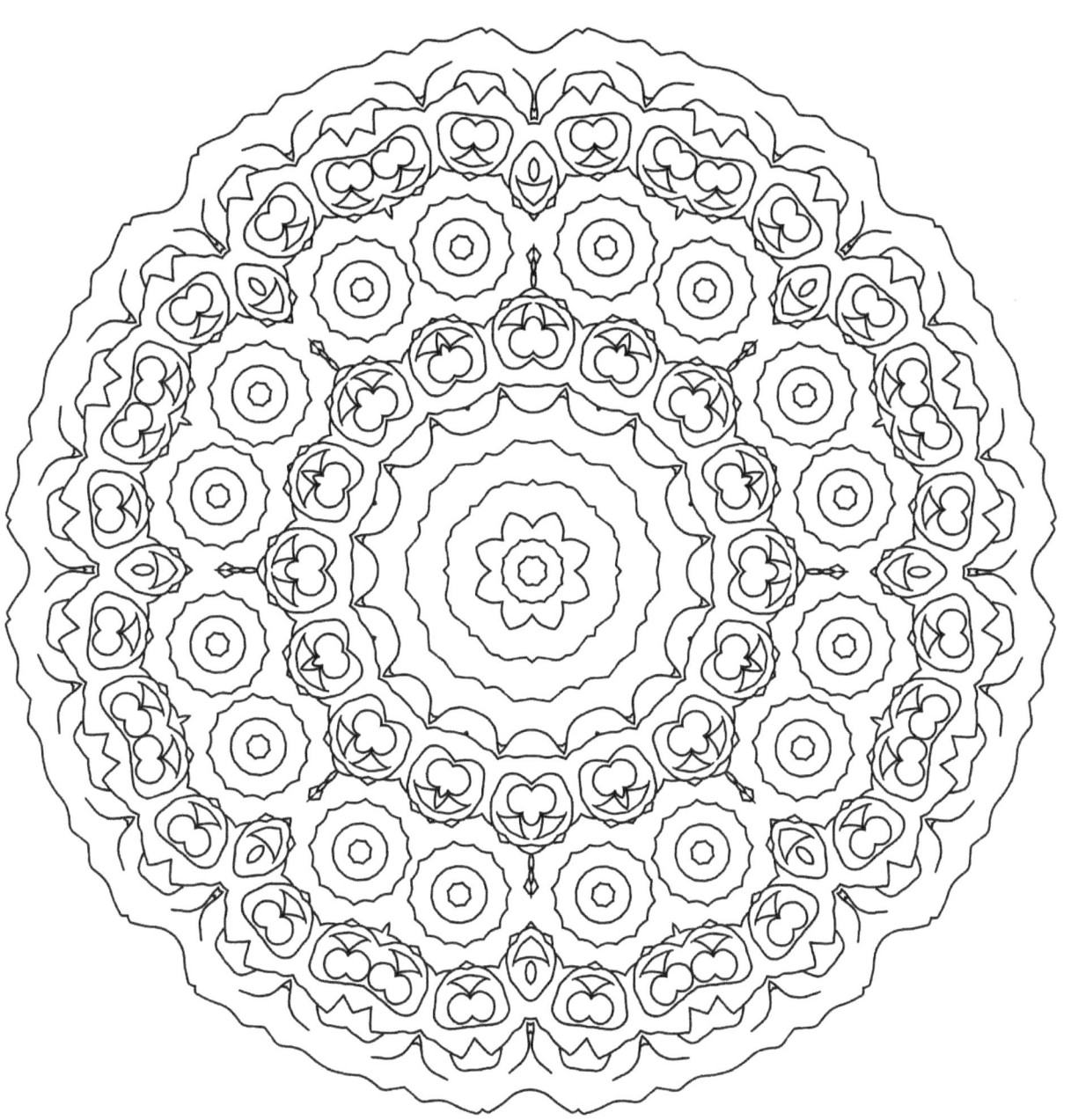

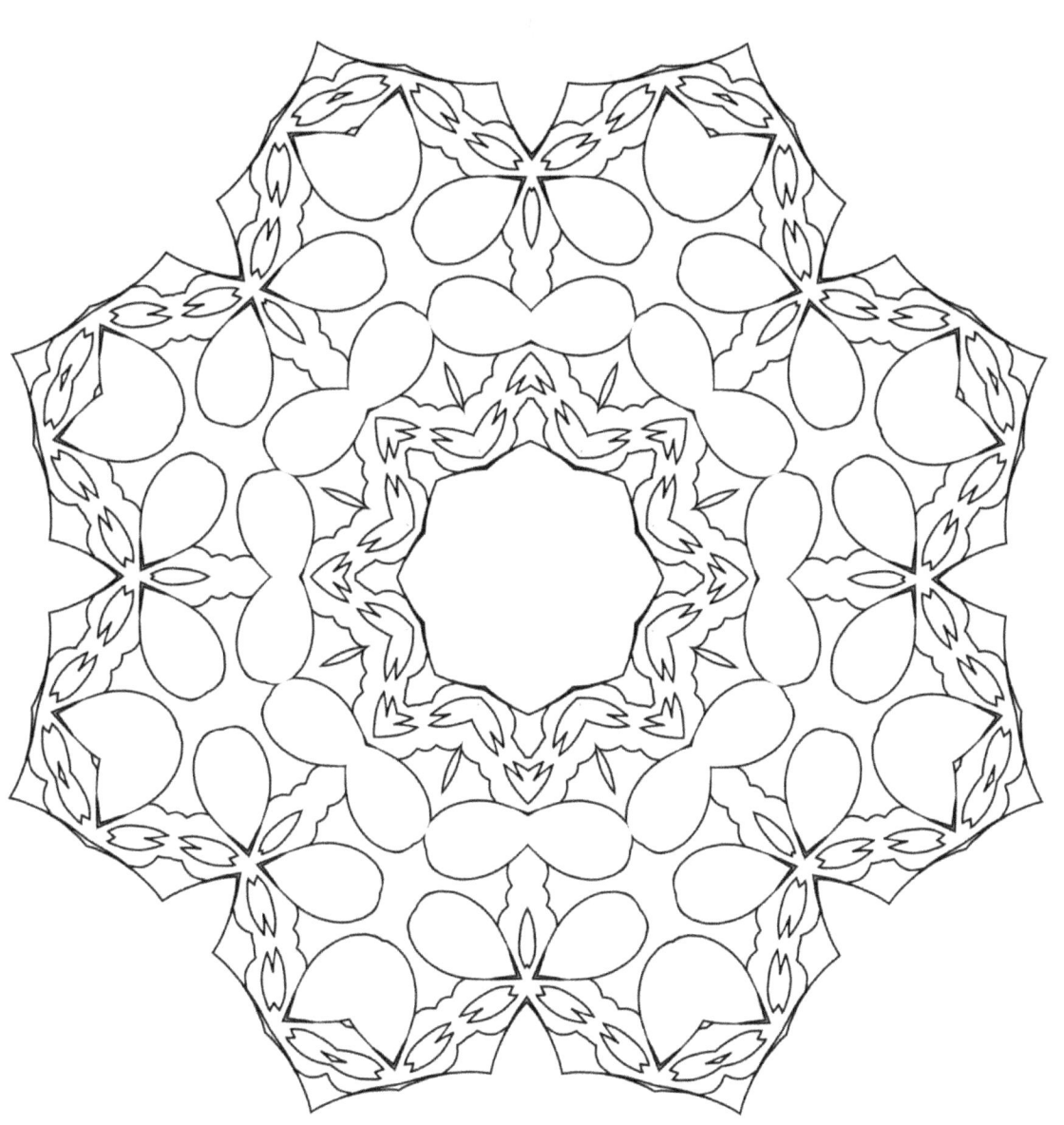

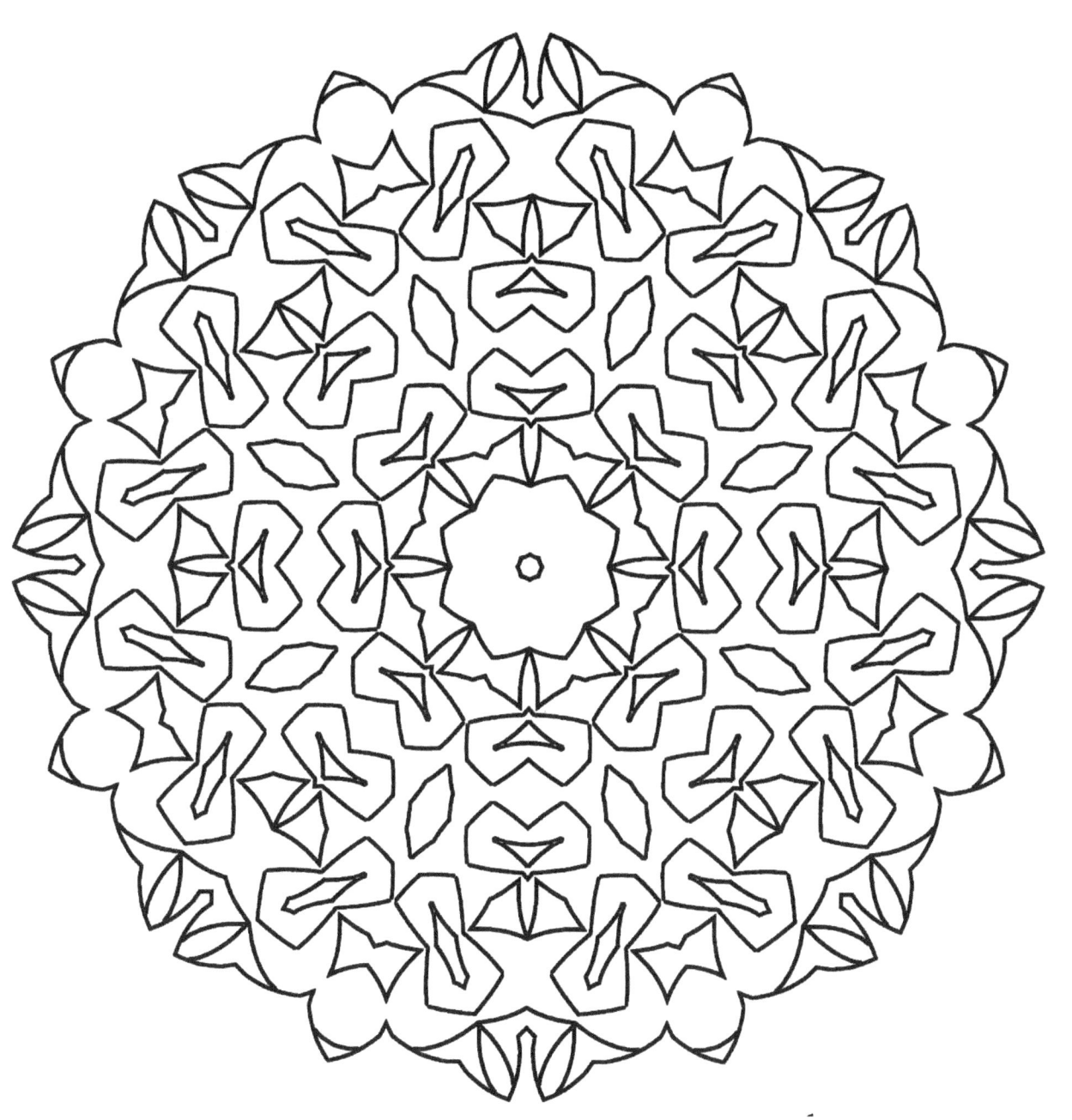

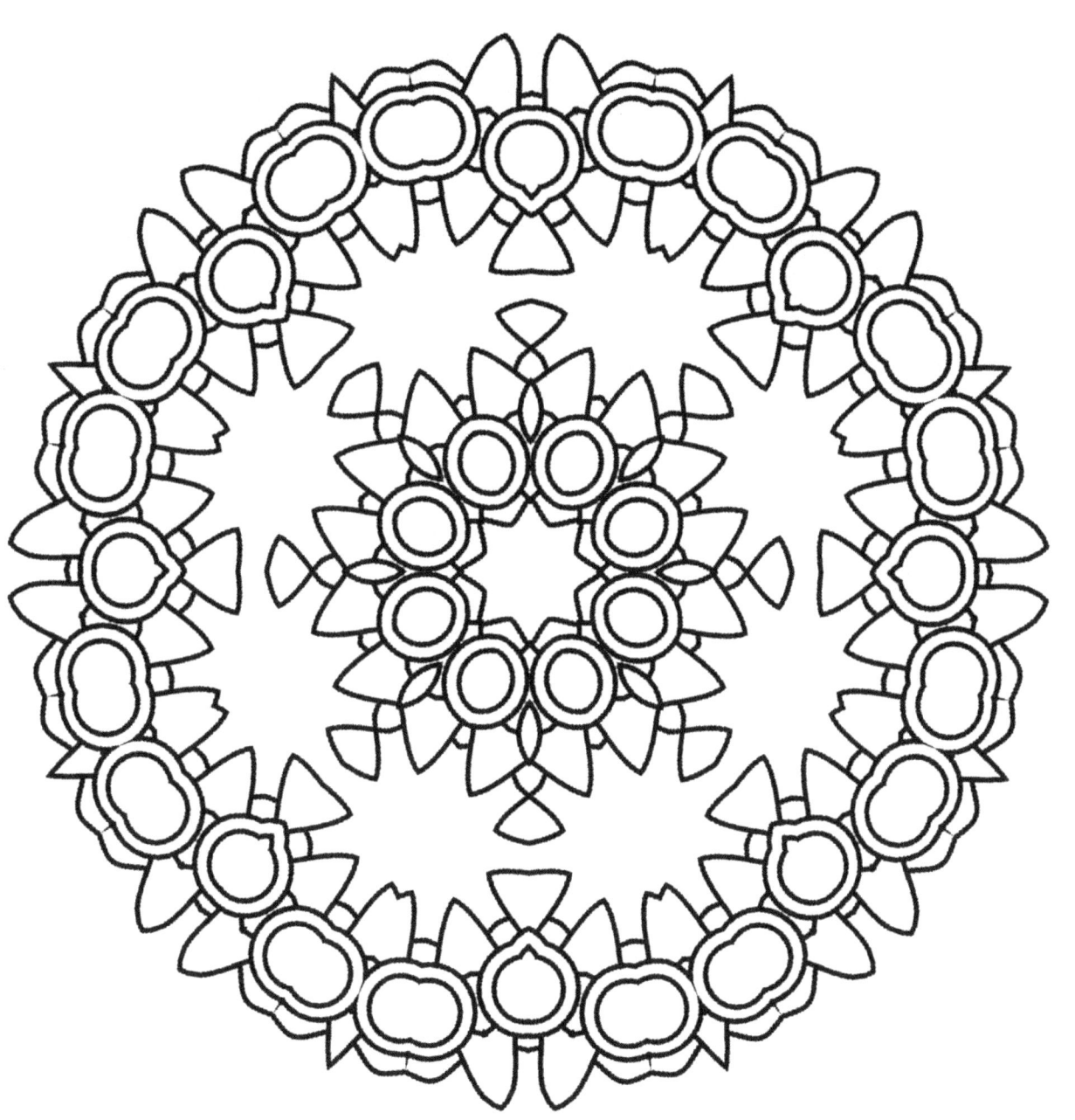

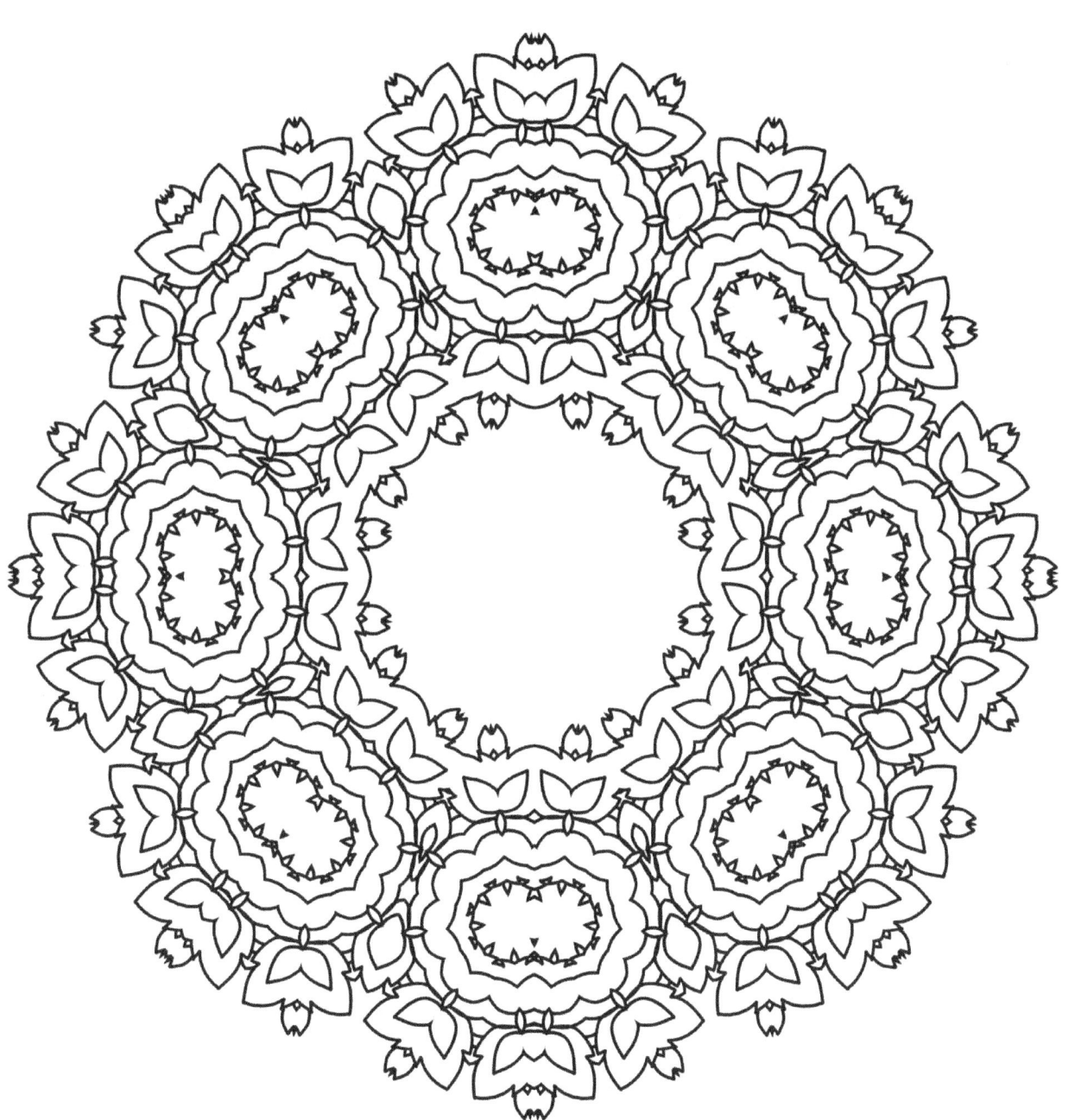

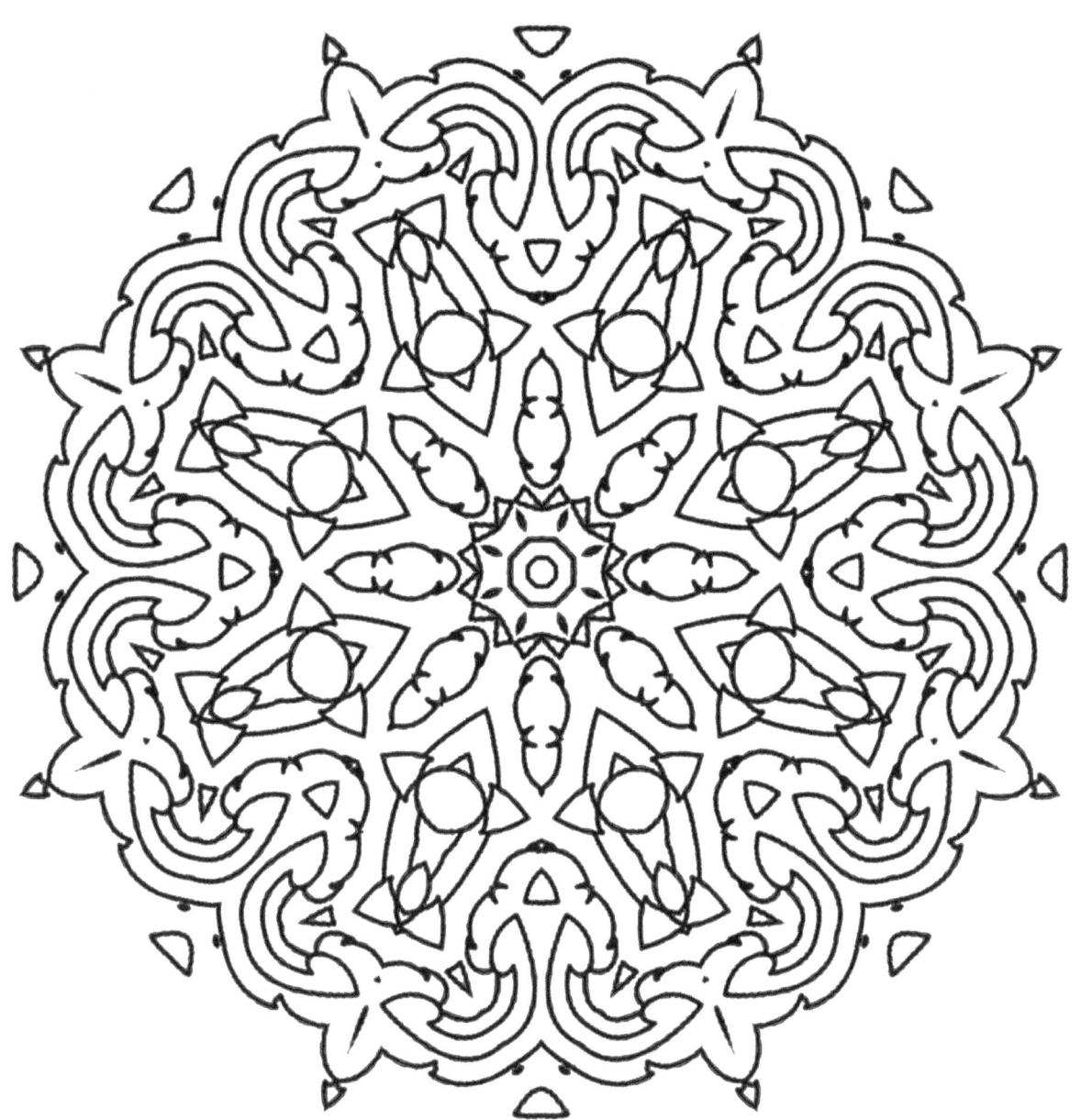

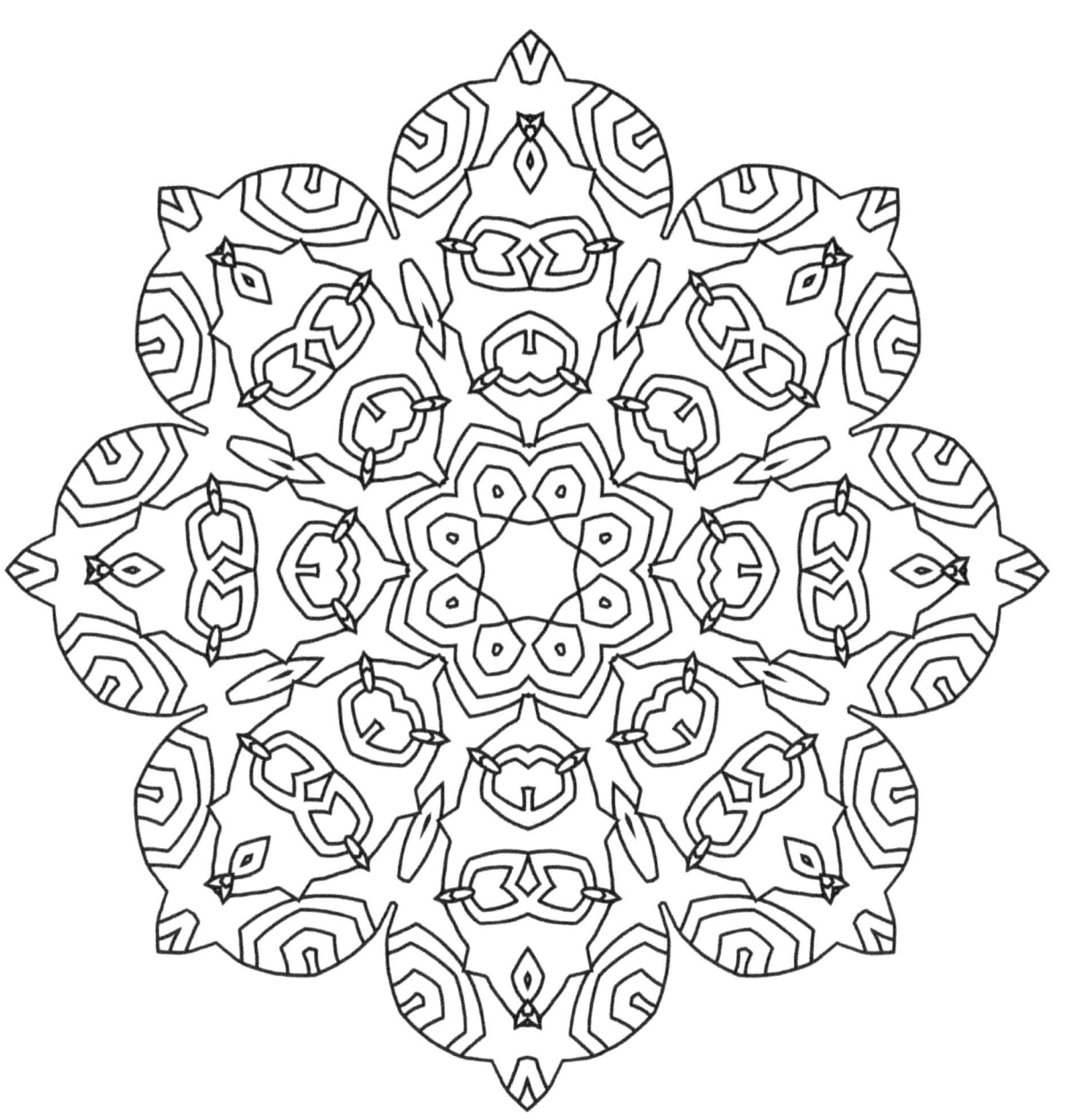

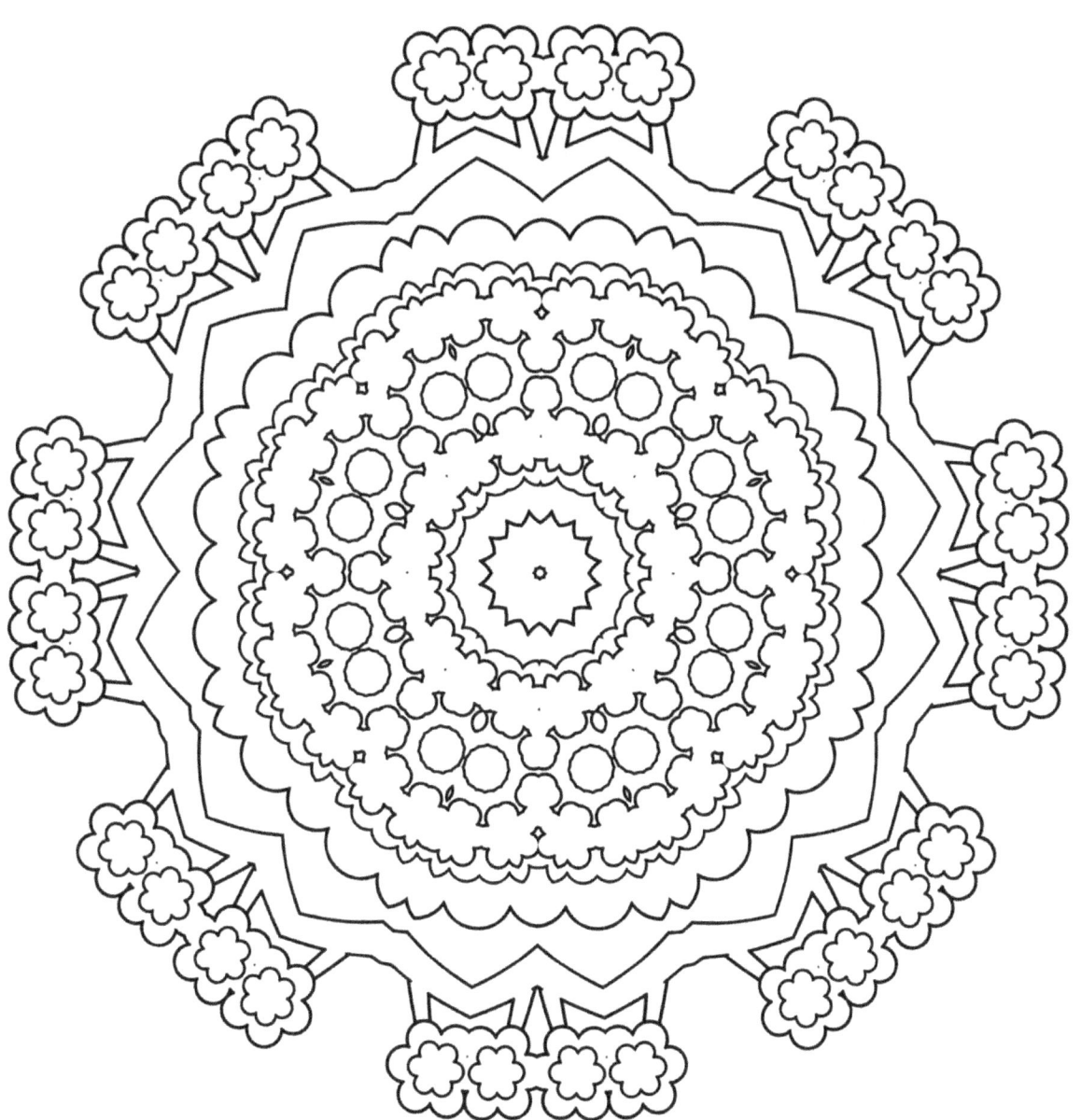

Thank you

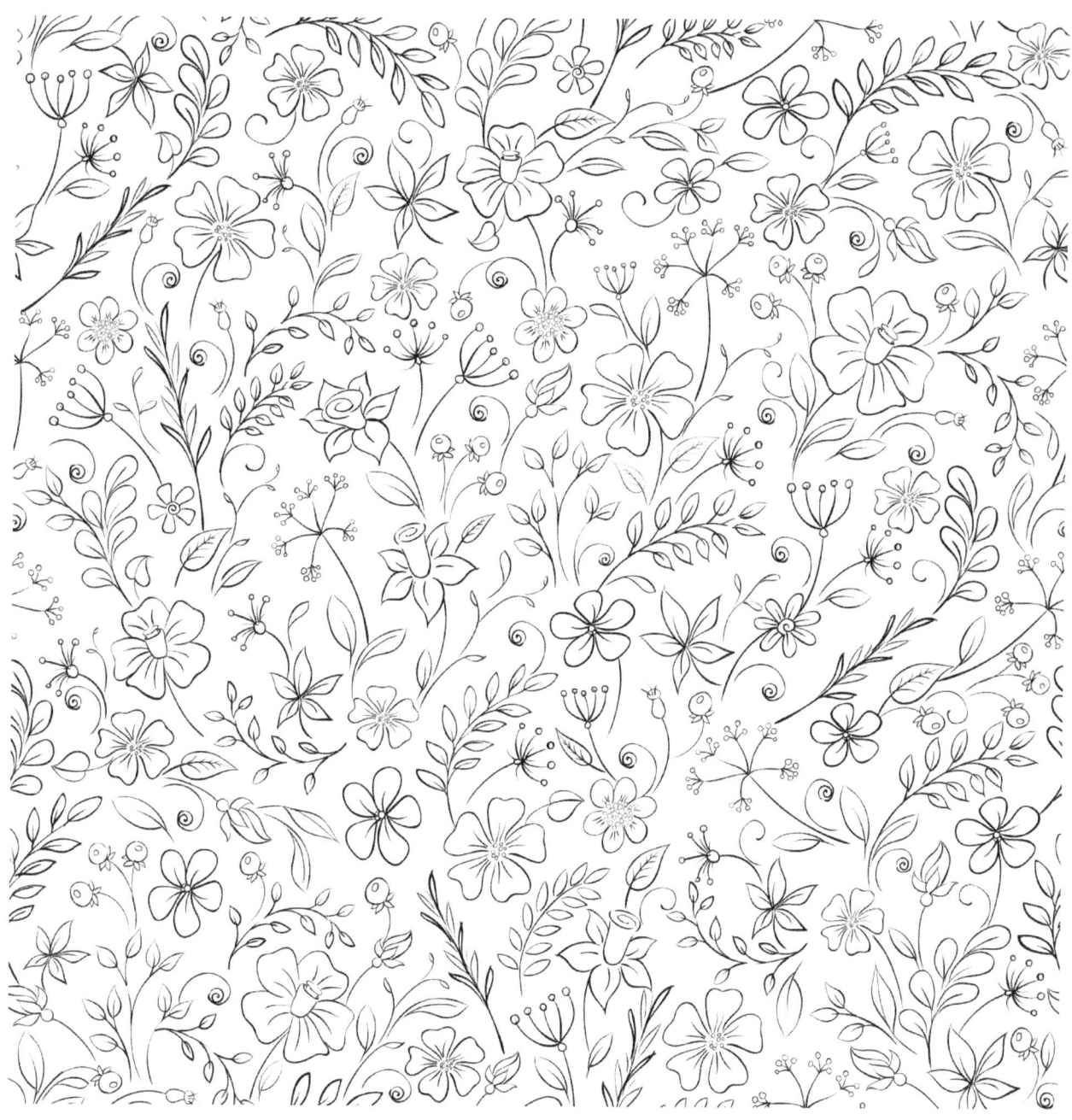

www.ingramcontent.com/pod-product-compliance
Lightning Source LLC
Chambersburg PA
CBHW080621190526
45169CB00009B/3256